EDUCATION IN A COMPETITIVE AND GLOBALIZING WORLD SERIES

EVALUATING ONLINE LEARNING: CHALLENGES AND STRATEGIES FOR SUCCESS

EDUCATION IN A COMPETITIVE AND GLOBALIZING WORLD SERIES

Motivation in Education
Desmond H. Elsworth (Editor)
2009. ISBN: 978-1-60692-234-7

The Reading Literacy of U.S. Fourth-Grade Students in an International Context
Justin Baer, Stéphane Baldi, Kaylin Ayotte,Patricia J. Green and Daniel McGrath
2009 ISBN: 978-1-60692-138-3

Teacher Qualifications and Kindergartners Achievements
Cassandra M. Guarino, Laura S. Hamilton, J.R. Lockwood,Amy H. Rathbun and Elvira Germino Hausken
2009 ISBN: 978-1-60741-180-2

Effects of Family Literacy Interventions on Children's Acquisition of Reading
Ana Carolina Pena (Editor)
2009 ISBN: 978-1-60741-236-6

Nutrition Education and Change
Beatra F. Realine (Editor)
2009. ISBN: 978-1-60692-983-4

Reading at Risk: A Survey of Literary Reading in America
Rainer D. Ivanov
2009. ISBN: 978-1-60692-582-9

Evaluating Online Learning: Challenges and Strategies for Success
Arthur T. Weston (Editor)
2009. ISBN: 978-1-60741-107-9

EDUCATION IN A COMPETITIVE AND GLOBALIZING WORLD SERIES

EVALUATING ONLINE LEARNING: CHALLENGES AND STRATEGIES FOR SUCCESS

ARTHUR T. WESTON
EDITOR

Nova Science Publishers, Inc.
New York

For permission to use material from this book please contact us:
Telephone 631-231-7269; Fax 631-231-8175
Web Site: http://www.novapublishers.com

LIBRARY OF CONGRESS CATALOGING-IN-PUBLICATION DATA
Available upon request
ISBN: 978-1-60741-107-9

Published by Nova Science Publishers, Inc. ✢ New York

CONTENTS

PREFACE

Education in this country has evolved dramatically from the days of one teacher in a one-room schoolhouse. Today, student learning is no longer confined to a physical space. Computers and the Internet have broken through school walls, giving students greater opportunities to personalize their education, access distant resources, receive extra help or more-challenging assignments, and engage in learning in new and unique ways. This book provides a new look at the relatively new enterprise of online learning in the K–12 arena, which is expanding rapidly, with increasing numbers of providers offering services and more students choosing to participate. As with any education program, online learning initiatives must be held accountable for results. Thus, it is critical for students and their parents, as well as administrators, policymakers, and funders to have data informing them about program and student outcomes and, if relevant, about how well a particular program compares to traditional education models. Rigorous evaluations are essential to this process and are included in this book. They identify whether programs and online resources are performing as promised, and equally important, they can point to areas for improvement.

This is an edited, reformatted and augmented edition of an Innovations in Education publication, prepared by WestEd with Edvance Research, Inc. for U.S. Department of Education, Office of Innovation and Improvement, 2008.

FOREWORD

Education in this country has evolved dramatically from the days of one teacher in a one-room schoolhouse. today, student learning is no longer confined to a physical space. Computers and the Internet have broken through school walls, giving students greater opportunities to personalize their education, access distant resources, receive extra help or more-challenging assignments, and engage in learning in new and unique ways.

Although online learning is a relatively new enterprise in the K–12 arena, it is expanding rapidly, with increasing numbers of providers offering services and more students choosing to participate. as with any education program, online learning initiatives must be held accountable for results. thus, it is critical for students and their parents—as well as administrators, policymakers, and funders—to have data informing them about program and student outcomes and, if relevant, about how well a particular program compares to traditional education models. to this end, rigorous evaluations are essential. they can identify whether programs and online resources are performing as promised, and, equally important, they can point to areas for improvement.

The evaluations highlighted in this guide represent a broad spectrum of online options, from programs that provide online courses to Web sites that feature education resources. the evaluations themselves range from internal assessments to external, scientific research studies. all demonstrate how program leaders and evaluators have been able to implement strong evaluation practices despite some challenges inherent to examining learning in an online environment.

This guide complements another publication, *Connecting Students to Advanced Courses Online*, published last year by the u.S. department of Education. Both are part of the Innovations in Education series, which identifies examples of innovative practices from across the country that are helping students achieve.

My hope is that this guide will assist evaluators and program leaders who seek to use data to guide program improvement aimed at achieving positive outcomes for our nation's students.

Margaret Spellings,
Secretary
U.S. department of Education

ACKNOWLEDGMENTS

This guide was developed under the auspices of the u.S. Department of Education's Office of Innovation and Improvement. Sharon Horn was project director.

An external advisory group provided feedback to refine the study scope, define the selection criteria, and clarify the text. Members included Robert Blomeyer, president, Blomeyer & Clemente Consulting Services; Tom Clark, president, TA Consulting; Trina Davis, president, International Society for Technology in Education, and assistant professor and director of eEducation, Texas A&M university; Helene Jennings, vice president, Macro International, Inc.; Liz Pape, president and chief executive officer of virtual High School Global Consortium; and Lisa Evans, director, Center for Evaluation Capacity Building, Wexford, Inc.

Staff in the Department of Education who provided input and reviewed drafts include Sue Betka, Cynthia Cabell, Tom Corwin, Kate Devine, David Dunn, Lorenzo Esters, Meredith Farace, Steve Fried, Cheryl Garnette, virginia Gentles, Robin Gilchrist, Doug Herbert, Nettie Laster, Brian Lekander, Meghan Lerch, Tiffany Taber, Linda Wilson, and Jacquelyn Zimmermann. This guide would not be possible without the support of Tim Magner, director, Office of Educational Technology.

The seven online programs that participated in the development of this guide and the case studies on which it is based were generous with both their time and attention.

Alabama Connecting Classrooms, Educators, & Students Statewide Distance Learning
Alabama Department of Education

50 N. Ripley St.
P.O. Box 302101
Montgomery, AL 36104
http://accessdl.state.al.us

Algebra I Online
Louisiana virtual School
Louisiana Department of Education
P.O. Box 94064
Baton Rouge, LA 70804-9064
http://www.louisianavirtualschool.net/?algebra

Appleton eSchool
2121 E. Emmers Drive
Appleton, WI 54915 http://www.aasd.k12.wi.us/Eschool

Arizona Virtual Academy
4595 S. Palo verde Road
Suite 517/519
Tucson, AZ 85714
http://www.azva.org

Chicago Public Schools' Virtual High School 125 S. Clark St.
Chicago, IL 60603 http://clear.cps.k12.il.us/ohsp/distance_ learning.html

Digital Learning Commons
Corbet Building
4507 university Way NE
Suite 204
Seattle, WA 98105 http://www.learningcommons.org

Thinkport
Maryland Public Television 11767 Owings Mills Blvd. Owings Mills, MD 21117 http://www.thinkport.org
in partnership with:
Johns Hopkins Center for Technology in Education
6740 Alexander Bell Drive
Suite 302
Columbia, MD 21046 http://cte.jhu.edu/index.htm

INTRODUCTION

This guide is designed as a resource for leaders and evaluators of K–12 online learning programs. In this guide the term "online learning" is used to refer to a range of education programs and resources in the K–12 arena, including distance learning courses offered by universities, private providers, or teachers at other schools; stand-alone "virtual schools" that provide students with a full array of online courses and services; and educational Web sites that offer teachers, parents, and students a range of resources.[1] The guide features seven evaluations that represent variety in both the type of program or resource being evaluated, and in the type of evaluation. These evaluations were selected because they offer useful lessons to others who are planning to evaluate an online learning program or resource.

Of course, evaluating online learning is not altogether different from assessing any other type of education program, and, to some degree, evaluators may face the same kind of design and analysis issues in both instances. Still, online program evaluators may encounter some unanticipated challenges in the virtual arena owing, for example, to the distance between program sites and students, participants' unfamiliarity with the technology being used, and a lack of relevant evaluation tools. this guide examines a range of challenges that online program evaluators are likely to meet, some that are unique to online settings and others that are more general. It also describes how online environments can sometimes offer advantages to evaluators by presenting opportunities for streamlined data collection and analysis, for example.

The guide specifically focuses on challenges and response strategies. All of the evaluations described here illustrate strong assessment practices and robust findings, and they are models for demonstrating how program leaders and evaluators can handle the challenges of evaluating online learning.

Common Challenges of Evaluating Online Learning

Online learning is a relatively new development in K–12 education but is rapidly expanding in both number of programs and participants. According to a report by the north American Council for Online Learning (nACOL), "As of September 2007, 42 states [had] significant supplemental online learning programs (in which students enrolled in physical schools take one or two courses online), or significant full-time programs (in which students take most or all of their courses online), or both."[2] In addition, the Internet houses an ever-expanding number of Web sites with a broad range of education resources for students, parents, and teachers. Given this expansion and a dearth of existing research on the topic, it is critical to conduct rigorous evaluations of online learning in K–12 settings to ensure that it does what people hope it will do: help improve student learning.

However, those undertaking such evaluations ay well encounter a number of technical and methodological issues that can make this type of research difficult to execute. For example, the scant research literature on K–12 online learning evaluation provides few existing frameworks to help evaluators describe and analyze programs, or tools, such as surveys or rubrics, they can use to collect data or assess program quality. Another common challenge when students are studying online is the difficulty of examining what is happening in multiple, geographically distant learning sites. And multifaceted education resources—such as vast Web sites offering a wide range of features or virtual schools that offer courses from multiple vendors—are also hard to evaluate, as are programs that utilize technologies and instructional models that are new to users.

Furthermore, evaluations of online learning often occur in the context of a politically loaded debate about whether such programs are worth the investment and how much funding is needed to run a high-quality program; about whether online learning really provides students with high-quality learning opportunities; and about how to compare online and traditional approaches. understandably, funders and policymakers—not to mention students and their parents—want data that show whether online learning can be as effective as traditional educational approaches and which online models are the best. these stakeholders may or may not think about evaluation in technical terms, but all of them are interested in how students perform in these new programs. At the same time, many online program leaders have multiple goals in mind, such as increased student engagement or increased student access to high-quality courses and teachers. they argue that test scores alone are an inadequate measure for capturing important differences between traditional and online learning settings. And, like educators in any setting—traditional or online—they may feel a natural trepidation about inviting evaluators to take a critical look at their program, fearing that it will hamper the progress of their program, rather than strengthen it.

This guide will discuss how evaluators have tried to compare traditional and online learning approaches, what challenges they have encountered, and what lessons they have learned.

THE FEATURED EVALUATIONS

This guide intentionally features a variety of online programs and resources, including virtual schools, programs that provide courses online, and Web sites with broad educational resources. Some serve an entire state, while others serve a particular district. this guide also includes distinct kinds of evaluations, from internally led formative evaluations (see Glossary of Common Evaluation terms, p. 65) to scientific research studies by external experts. In some cases, program insiders initiated the evaluations; in others, there were external reasons for the evaluation. the featured evaluations include a wide range of data collection and analysis activities—from formative evaluations that rely primarily on survey, interview, and observation data, to scientific experiments that compare outcomes between online and traditional settings. In each instance, evaluators chose the methods carefully, based on the purpose of the evaluation and the specific set of research questions they sought to answer.

The goal in choosing a range of evaluations for this guide was to offer examples that could be instructive to program leaders and evaluators in diverse circumstances, including those in varying stages of maturity, with varying degrees of internal capacity and amounts of available funding. the featured evaluations are not without flaws, but they all illustrate reasonable strategies for tackling common challenges of evaluating online learning.

To select the featured evaluations, researchers for this guide compiled an initial list of candidates by searching for K–12 online learning evaluations on the Web and in published documents, then expanded the list through referrals from a six-member advisory group (see list of members in the Acknowledgments section, p. vii) and other knowledgeable experts in the field. Forty organizations were on the final list for consideration.

A matrix of selection criteria was drafted and revised based on feedback from the advisory group. the three quality criteria were:

- the evaluation considered multiple outcome measures, including student achievement.
- the evaluation findings were widely communicated to key stakeholders of the program or resource being studied.
- Program leaders acted on evaluation results.

Researchers awarded sites up to three points on each of these three criteria, using publicly available information, review of evaluation reports, and gap-filling interviews with program leaders. All the included sites scored at least six of the possible nine points across these three criteria.

Since a goal of this publication was to showcase a variety of types of evaluations, the potential sites were coded as to such additional characteristics as: internal vs. external evaluator, type of evaluation design, type of online learning program or resource, whether the program serves a district- or state-level audience, and stage of maturity. In selecting the featured evaluations, the researchers drew from as wide a range of characteristics as possible while keeping the quality criteria high. A full description of the methodology used to study the evaluation(s) of the selected sites can be found in appendix B: Research Methodology.

The final selection included evaluations of the following online programs and resources: Alabama Connecting Classrooms, Educators, & Students Statewide distance Learning, operated by the Alabama department of Education; Algebra I Online, operated by the Louisiana department of Education; Appleton eSchool, operated by Wisconsin's Appleton Area School district; Arizona virtual Academy, a public charter school; Chicago Public Schools' virtual High School; digital Learning Commons in Washington state; and thinkport, a Web site operated by Maryland Public television and Johns Hopkins Center for technology in Education. Additional information about each program and its evaluation(s) is included in table 1.

WHAT'S IN THIS GUIDE

This guide was developed as a resource for evaluators, whether external, third-party researchers, or program administrators and other staff who are considering conducting their own internal evaluation. Some of the evaluations highlighted here were carried out by external evaluators, while others were conducted by program staff or the staff of a parent organization. In all cases, the research was undertaken by experienced professionals, and this publication is aimed primarily at readers who are familiar with basic evaluation practices. For readers who are less familiar with evaluation, a glossary of common terms is available on page 65.

Table 1. Selected Variables of Profiled Online Learning Evaluations

Name of Program or Resource	Type of Program or Resource/ Year Initiated	Type of Evaluation Featured in Guide[a]	Year Evalua- ion Started	Evaluation Objective
Alabama Connect- ing Classrooms, Educators, & Students Statewide Distance Learning	Online courses and interactive video-conference classes for students across state / Piloted in spring 2006; statewide imple-mentation in fall 2006	External; formative & summative; includes com-parisons with traditional instructional settings	2006	Monitoring program implementation; program improvement; sharing best practices
Algebra I Online	Online algebra courses for stu- dents across the state / 2002	External and internal; formative and summative; includes comparisons with traditional instructional settings	2003; com-parative study in 2004–05	Determine if program is effective way to provide stu-dents with certified algebra teachers and to support the in-class teacher's certification efforts
Appleton eSchool	Online courses for students en- rolled in district's high schools (some students take all courses online) / 2002	Internal; formative; evalua- tion process based on inter-nally developed rubric	Rubric piloted in 2006	Program improvement; sharing best practices
Arizona Virtual Academy	Virtual charter school for stu- dents enrolled in public schools and homeschool students (no more than 20%) / 2003	Formative and summative; external and internal	2003	State monitoring; quality assurance; program im-provement
Chicago Public Schools – Virtual High School	Online courses for students en- rolled in district's high schools / 2002	External; formative	2002	Assess need for mentor training and other student supports; identify ways to improve completion and pass rates

Table 1. Continued

Name of Program or Resource	Type of Program or Resource/ Year Initiated	Type of Evaluation Featured in Guide[a]	Year Evalua- ion Started	Evaluation Objective
Digital Learning Commons	Web site with online courses and a wide array of resources for teachers and students / 2003	External and internal; for- mative	2003	Understand usage of site; assess impact on student achievement and college readiness
Thinkport – Maryland Public Television with Johns Hopkins	Web site with a wide array of resources for teachers and students / 2000	External and internal; formative and summative, including randomized con- trolled trial	2001; randomize d controlled trial in 2005	Understand usage of site; assess impact of "electronic field trip" on student performance

[a] See Glossary of Common Evaluation Terms on page 65.

[b] Run by the nonprofit College Board, the Advanced Placement (AP) program offers college-level course work to high school students. Many institutions of higher education offer college credits to students who take AP courses.

[c] North Central Regional Educational Laboratory.

Cost of Evaluation	Funding Source for Evaluation	Data Collected	Data Collection Tools	Improvements Resulting From Evaluation
$60,000 in 2007; $600,000 in 2008	Specific allocation in program budget (originating from state of Alabama)	Student enrollment, comple- tion, grades; AP[b] course pass rates; student and teacher satisfaction; de- scription of implementation and challenges	Surveys, interviews, observations	Teacher professional development; improvements to technology and administrative operations
$1 10,000 for the most labor-intensive phase, including the comparative analysis during 2004–05	General program funds, grants from NCREL,[c] BellSouth Foundation, and U.S. Department of Education	Student grades and state test scores; pre- and post- tests; student use and satis- faction data; focus groups; teacher characteristics and teachers' certification outcomes	Pre- and posttests developed by eval- uator, surveys	Teacher professional develop- ment; increased role for in-class teachers, curriculum improve- ments, new technologies used; expansion to middle schools
No specific allocation; Approx. $15,000 to make the	General program funds (originating	Internal descriptions and as- sessments of key program components (using	Internally developed rubric and surveys	Mentor professional development; course content improve- ments; expanded

rubric and evaluation process available in Web format	from charter grant from state of Wis- consin)	rubric); mentor, student, and teacher satisfaction data; course completion and grades		interactivity in courses; improvements to pro- gram Web site and printed mate- rials; sharing of best practices
No specific allocation	General program funds (originating from state of Ari- zona)	Student enrollment, grades, and state test scores; par- ent, teacher, and student satisfaction data; internal & external assessments on key program components	Electronic surveys; externally devel- oped rubric	Wide range of operational and instructional improvements
Approx. $25,000	District's Office of Technology Services	Student enrollment, course completion, grades, and test scores; student use and satisfaction data; mentor assessments of needs	Surveys, interviews, focus groups	Designated class periods for online learning; more onsite mentors; training for mentors
Approx. $80,000 for the college-readiness study	Bill & Melinda Gates Foundation	Student transcripts; student grades and completion rates; use and satisfaction data	Surveys	Improvements to student orientation; curriculum improve- ments; development of school use plans to encourage best practices
Estimated $40,000 for the randomized controlled trial (part of a comprehensive evaluation)	Star Schools Grant	Student test scores on custom-developed content assessment; information about delivery of curriculum; use and satisfaction data	Test of content knowl- edge developed by evaluator, surveys, teacher implementa- tion logs	Changes to teaching materials; changes to online content and format

Part I of this guide focuses on some of the likely challenges faced by online program evaluators, and it is organized into the following sections:

- Meeting the needs of Multiple Stakeholders
- Building on the Existing Base of Knowledge
- Evaluating Multifaceted Online Resources
- Finding appropriate Comparison Groups
- Solving data Collection Problems
- Interpreting the Impact of Program Maturity
- translating Evaluation Findings Into action

Each section of Part I presents practical information about one of the challenges of evaluating online learning and provides examples of how the featured evaluations have addressed it. Part II synthesizes the lessons learned from meeting those challenges and offers recommendations based as well on research and conversations with experts in evaluating online learning. these are geared to program leaders who are considering an evaluation and to assist them and their evaluators as they work together to design and complete the process. Brief profiles of each of the seven online programs can be found at the end of the guide, and details about each evaluation are summarized in table 1.

PART I. CHALLENGES OF EVALUATING ONLINE LEARNING

In: Evaluating Online Learning
Editor: Arthur T. Weston, pp. 16-21
ISBN 978-1-60741-107-9

Chapter 1

MEETING THE NEEDS OF MULTIPLE STAKEHOLDERS

Every good evaluation begins with a clearly stated purpose and a specific set of questions to be answered. these questions drive the evaluation approach and help determine the specific data collection techniques that evaluators will use. Sometimes, however, program evaluators find themselves in the difficult position of needing to fulfill several purposes at once, or needing to answer a wide variety of research questions. Most stakeholders have the same basic question—Is it working? But not everyone defines *working* in the same way. While policymakers may be interested in gains in standardized test scores, program leaders may be equally interested in other indicators of success, such as whether the program is addressing the needs of traditionally underrepresented subgroups, or producing outcomes that are only indirectly related to test scores, like student engagement.

Naturally, these questions will not be answered in the same way. For example, if stakeholders want concrete evidence about the impact on student achievement, evaluators might conduct a randomized controlled trial—the gold standard for assessing program effects—or a quasi- experimental design that compares test scores of program participants with students in matched

Comparison groups. But if stakeholders want to know, for example, *how* a program has been implemented across many sites, or *why* it is leading to particular outcomes, then they might opt for a descriptive study, incorporating such techniques as surveys, focus groups, or observations of program participants to gather qualitative process data.

When multiple stakeholders have differing interests and questions, how can evaluators meet these various expectations?

To satisfy the demands of multiple stakeholders, evaluators often combine formative and summative components (see Glossary of Common Evaluation terms, p. 65). In the case of Alabama Connecting Classrooms, Educators, & Students Statewide distance Learning (ACCESS), described below, the evaluators have been very proactive in designing a series of evaluations that, collectively, yield information that has utility both for program improvement and for understanding program performance. In the case of Arizona virtual Academy (AZvA), the school's leadership team has made the most of the many evaluation activities they are required to complete by using findings from those activities for their own improvement purposes and piggybacking on them with data collection efforts of their own. In each instance, program leaders would likely say that their evaluations are first and foremost intended to improve their programs. Yet, when called upon to show achievement results, they can do that as well.

Combine Formative and Summative Evaluation Approaches to Meet Multiple Demands

From the beginning of their involvement with ACCESS, evaluators from the International Society for technology in Education (IStE) have taken a combined summative and formative approach to studying this state-run program that offers both Web-based and interactive videoconferencing courses. the original development proposal for ACCESS included an accountability plan that called for ongoing monitoring of the program to identify areas for improvement and to generate useful information that could be shared with other schools throughout the state. In addition, from the beginning, program leaders and state policymakers expressed interest in gathering data about the program's impact on student learning. to accomplish these multiple goals, IStE completed two successive evaluations for Alabama, each of which had both formative and summative components. A third evaluation is under way.

The first evaluation, during the program's pilot implementation, focused on providing feedback that could be used to modify the program, if need be, and on generating information to share with Alabama schools. Evaluation activities at this stage included a literature review and observation visits to six randomly selected pilot sites, where evaluators conducted interviews and surveys. they also ran focus groups, for which researchers interviewed respondents in a group settincation about how the pilot program was being implemented and what changes might be needed to strengthen it.

The second evaluation took more of a summative approach, looking to see whether or not ACCESS was meeting its overall objectives. First, evaluators conducted surveys and interviews of students and teachers, as well as interviews with school administrators and personnel at the program's three Regional Support Centers. In addition, they gathered student enrollment and achievement data, statewide course enrollment and completion rates, and other program outcome data, such as the number of new distance courses developed and the number of participating schools.

This second evaluation also used a quasi-experimental design (see Glossary of Common Evaluation terms, p. 65) to provide information on program effects. Evaluators compared achievement outcomes between ACCESS participants and students statewide, between students in interactive videoconferencing courses and students in traditional settings, and between students who participated in online courses and those who took courses offered in the interactive videoconferencing format.

As of early 2008, the evaluators were conducting a third evaluation, integrating the data from the first two studies and focusing on student achievement. Looking ahead, ACCESS leaders plan to continue gathering data annually in anticipation of conducting longitudinal studies that will identify ACCESS's full impact on student progress and achievement.

Together, the carefully planned evaluation activities conducted by ACCESS's evaluators have generated several findings and recommendations that already have been used to strengthen the program. For example, their findings suggest that students participating in the distance learning courses are completing courses at high rates and, in the case of the College Board Advanced Placement (AP) courses,[3] are achieving scores comparable to students taught in traditional settings. these kinds of data could be critical to maintaining funding and political support for the program in the future. ACCESS also is building a longitudinal database to provide a core of data for use in future evaluations and, program leaders hope, to help determine ACCESS's long-term impact on student progress and achievement. With these data collection tools and processes in place, ACCESS has armed itself to address the needs and expectations of various stakeholders inside and outside the program.

Reasons and Contexts for Formative Versus Summative Evaluations

Formative and summative evaluations can each serve important functions for programs. Formative evaluations, sometimes called "process evaluations," are conducted primarily to find out how a program is being implemented and how it might be strengthened. Summative evaluations, also called "outcome evaluations," are appropriate for better-established programs, when program leaders have settled on their best policies and practices and want to know, for example, what results the program is yielding.

Ideally, formative evaluations are developed as partnerships that give all stakeholders a hand in planning and helping conduct the evaluation. Explicitly framing a formative evaluation as a collaboration among stakeholders can help in more ways than one. Practitioners are more likely to cooperate with and welcome evaluators rather than feel wary or threatened—a common reaction. In addition, practitioners who are invited to be partners in an evaluation are more likely to feel invested in its results and to implement the findings and recommendations.

Even more than formative evaluations, summative evaluations can be perceived by practitioners as threatening and, in many cases, program staff are not eager to welcome evaluators into their midst. Even in these situations, however, their reaction can be mitigated if evaluators work diligently to communicate the evaluation's goals. Evaluators should make clear their intention to provide the program with information that can be used to strengthen it, or to give the program credible data to show funders or other stakeholders. In many cases, summative evaluations do not uncover findings that are unexpected; they merely provide hard data to back up the anecdotes and hunches of program leaders and staff.

Program leaders who are contemplating an evaluation also will want to consider the costs of whatever type of study they choose. Some formative evaluations are relatively informal. For example, a formative evaluation might consist primarily of short-term activities conducted by internal staff, like brief surveys of participants, to gather feedback about different aspects of the program. This type of evaluation is inexpensive and can be ideal for leaders seeking ongoing information to strengthen their program. In other instances, formative evaluation is more structured and formal. For instance, an external evaluator may be hired to observe or interview program participants, or to conduct field surveys and analyze the data. Having an external evaluator can bring increased objectivity, but it also adds cost.

In many cases, summative evaluations are more formal and expensive operations, particularly if they are using experimental or quasi-experimental designs that require increased coordination and management and sophisticated data analysis techniques. Typically, external evaluators conduct summative evaluations, which generally extends the timeline and ups the costs. Still, experimental and quasi-experimental designs may provide the most reliable information about program effects.

Finally, program leaders should consider that an evaluation need not be exclusively formative or summative. As the ACCESS case illustrates (see pp. 7–10), sometimes it is best for programs to combine elements of both, either concurrently or in different years.

MAKE THE MOST OF MANDATORY PROGRAM EVALUATIONS

While all leaders and staff of online education programs are likely to want to understand their influence on student learning, some have no choice in the matter. Many online programs must deliver summative student outcome data because a funder or regulatory body demands it. In the case of Arizona virtual Academy (AZvA), a K–1 2 statewide public charter school, the program must comply with several mandatory evaluation requirements: First, school leaders are required by the state of Arizona to submit an annual effectiveness review, which is used to determine whether or not the school's charter will be renewed. For this yearly report, AZvA staff must provide data on student enrollment, retention, mobility, and state test performance. the report also must include pupil and parent satisfaction data, which AZvA collects online at the end of each course, and a detailed self-evaluation of operational and administrative efficiency.

AZVA also must answer to K12 Inc., the education company that supplies the program's curriculum for all grade levels. K12 Inc. has its own interest in evaluating how well its curriculum products are working and in ensuring that it is partnered with a high-quality school. AZvA's director, Mary Gifford, says that "from the second you open your school," there is an expectation [on the part of K12 Inc.] that you will collect data, analyze them, and use them to make decisions. "K12 Inc. has established best practices for academic achievement. they take great pride in being a data-driven company," she adds. It conducts quality assurance audits at AZvA approximately every two years, which consist of a site visit conducted by K1 2 Inc. personnel and an extensive questionnaire, completed by AZvA, that documents various aspects of the program, such as instruction, organizational structure, and parent-school relations. K12 Inc. also requires AZvA to produce a detailed annual School Improvement Plan (SIP), which covers program operations as well as student achievement. the plan must include an analysis of student performance on standardized state tests, including a comparison of the performance of AZvA students to the performance of all students across the state.

Each of these mandates—those of the state and those of AZvA's curriculum provider—has an important purpose. But the multiple requirements add up to what could be seen as a substantial burden for any small organization. AZvA's small central staff chooses to look at it differently. Although the requirements generate year-round work for AZvA employees, they have made the most of these activities by using them for their own purposes, too. Each of the many mandated evaluation activities serves an internal purpose: Staff members pore over test scores, course completion data, and user satisfaction data to determine how they can improve their program. the SIP is used as a guiding document to organize information about what aspects of the program need fixing and to monitor the school's progress toward its stated goals. although the process is time-consuming, everyone benefits: K12 Inc. is assured that the school is doing what it should, aZva has a structured approach to improving its program, and it can demonstrate to the state and others that student performance is meeting expectations.

Azva is able to make the most of its mandatory evaluations because the school's culture supports it: Staff members incorporate data collection and analysis into their everyday responsibilities, rather than viewing them as extra burdens on their workload. Furthermore, aZva's leaders initiate data collection and analysis efforts of their own. they frequently conduct online surveys of parents to gauge the effectiveness of particular services. More recently, they also have begun to survey teachers about their professional development needs and their satisfaction with the trainings provided to them. "We're trying to do surveys after every single professional development [session], to find out what was most effective," says Gifford. "Do they want more of this, less of this? Was this too much time? Was this enough time? that feedback has been very good." aZva's K–8 principal, Bridget Schleifer, confirms that teachers' responses to the surveys are taken very seriously. "Whenever a survey comes up and we see a need," she says, "we will definitely put that on the agenda for the next month of professional development."

Together, these many efforts provide aZva with comprehensive information that helps the school address external accountability demands, while also serving internal program improvement objectives. Just as important, aZva's various evaluation activities are integrated and support each other. For instance, the SIP is based on the findings from the evaluation activities mandated by the state and

K12 Inc., and the latter's audit process includes an update on progress made toward SIP goals. More broadly, the formative evaluation activities help the school leaders to set specific academic goals and develop a plan for reaching them, which ultimately helps them improve the achievement outcomes assessed by the state. One lesson aZva illustrates is how to make the most of evaluations that are initiated externally by treating every data collection activity as an opportunity to learn something valuable that can serve the program.

SUMMARY

As the above program evaluations demonstrate, sometimes the best approach to meeting the needs of multiple stakeholders is being proactive. the steps are straightforward but critical: When considering an evaluation, program leaders should first identify the various stakeholders who will be interested in the evaluation and what they will want to know. they might consider conducting interviews or focus groups to collect this information. Leaders then need to sift through this information and prioritize their assessment goals. they should develop a clear vision for what they want their evaluation to do and work with evaluators to choose an evaluation type that will meet their needs. If it is meant to serve several different stakeholder groups, evaluators and program leaders might decide to conduct a multi-method study that combines formative and summative evaluation activities. they might also consider developing a multiyear evaluation plan that addresses separate goals in different years. In the reporting phase, program leaders and evaluators can consider communicating findings to different stakeholder audiences in ways that are tailored to their needs and interests.

In instances where online programs participate in mandatory evaluations, program leaders should seek to build on these efforts and use them for internal purposes as well. they can leverage the information learned in a summative evaluation to improve the program, acquire funding, or establish the program's credibility. Evaluators can help program leaders piggyback on any mandatory assessment activities by selecting complementary evaluation methods that will provide not just the required data but also information that program staff can use for their own improvement purposes.

In: Evaluating Online Learning
Editor: Arthur T. Weston, pp. 23-34
ISBN 978-1-60741-107-9

Chapter 2

BUILDING ON THE EXISTING BASE OF KNOWLEDGE

Under normal circumstances, evaluators frequently begin their work by reviewing available research literature. they also may search for a conceptual framework among similar studies or look for existing data collection tools, such as surveys and rubrics, that can be borrowed or adapted. Yet, compared to many other topics in K–1 2 education, the body of research literature on K–12 online learning is relatively new and narrow. Available descriptive studies are often very specific and offer findings that are not easily generalized to other online programs or resources. Empirical studies are few. Other kinds of tools for evaluators are limited, too. Recent efforts have led to multiple sets of standards for K–12 online learning (see Standards for K–12 Online Learning, p. 13). However, there still are no widely accepted education program outcome measures, making it difficult for evaluators to gauge success relative to other online or traditional programs.

Given the existing base of knowledge on K–12 online learning, how should evaluators proceed? Of course, evaluators will first want to consult the K–12 online learning research that does exist. Although the field is comparatively limited, it is growing each year and already has generated a number of significant resources (see appendix A, p. 59). Among other organizations, the north American Council for Online Learning (nACOL) has developed and collected dozens of publications, research studies, and other resources useful for evaluators of K–12 online learning programs. In some cases, evaluators also may want to look to higher education organizations, which have a richer literature on online learning evaluation, including several publications that identify standards and best practices (see appendix A). In some cases, these resources can be adapted for K–12 settings, but in other cases, researchers have found, they do not translate well.

Another approach is to develop evaluation tools and techniques from scratch. As described below, this may be as simple as defining and standardizing the outcome measures used among multiple schools or vendors, like the evaluators of digital Learning Commons did. Or it may be a much more ambitious effort, as when Appleton eSchool's leaders developed a new model for evaluating virtual schools with an online system for compiling evaluation data. Finally, some evaluators respond to a limited knowledge base by adding to it. For example, the evaluators of Louisiana's Algebra I Online program have published their evaluation findings for the benefit of other evaluators and program administrators.

In a different but equally helpful fashion, the leaders of Appleton eSchool have contributed to the field, by developing a Web site that allows administrators of online programs to share their best practices in a public forum.

Standards for K–12 Online Learning

As online learning in K–1 2 education has expanded, there has been an effort to begin to codify current best practices into a set of standards that educators can look to in guiding their own performance. Several organizations have released sets of these emerging standards based on practitioner input to date.

In late 2006, the Educational Technology Cooperative of the Southern Regional Education Board (SREB) issued Standards for Quality Online Courses. These standards are available along with other key resources from SREB at http://www.sreb.org/programs/EdTech/SVS/index.asp.

A year later, NACOL published National Standards of Quality for Online Courses, which endorsed SREB's standards and added a few others. The national standards cover six broad topic areas: course content, instructional design, student assessment, technology, course evaluation and management, and 21st-century skills.

NACOL also developed National Standards for Quality Online Teaching in 2008 and is currently working on program standards. The standards for online courses and teaching can be found at http://www.nacol.org along with many other resources.

The National Education Association also has published standards for online courses and online teachers, both available at http://www.nea.org.

Clearly Define Outcome Measures

Evaluators must be able to clearly articulate key program goals, define outcomes that align with them, and then identify specific outcome measures that can be used to track the program's progress in meeting the goals. Presently, however, outcome measures for evaluating online learning programs are not consistently defined, which makes it difficult for stakeholders to gauge a program's success, compare it to other programs, or set improvement goals that are based on the experience of other programs. Furthermore, the lack of consistent outcome measures creates technical headaches for evaluators. A recent article coauthored by Liz Pape, president and chief executive officer of virtual High School Global Consortium, a nonprofit network of online schools, describes the problem this way:

> Although standards for online course and program effectiveness have been identified, data-driven yardsticks for measuring against those standards are not generally agreed upon or in use. There is no general agreement about what to measure and how to measure. Even for measures that most programs use, such as course completion rates, there is variation in the metrics because the online programs that measure course completion rates do not measure in the same manner.[4]

The evaluators of Washington state's digital Learning Commons (dLC) encountered just such a problem when attempting to calculate the number of online course-takers served by the program. dLC is a centrally hosted Web portal that offers a wide range of online courses from numerous private vendors. When evaluators from Cohen Research and Evaluation tried to analyze dLC's course-taking and completion rates, they found a range of reporting practices among the vendors: Some tracked student participation throughout the course, while others reported only on the number of students who completed a course and received a final grade. Also, in some cases, vendors did not differentiate between students who withdrew from a course and students who received an F, conflating two different student outcomes that might have distinct implications for program improvement.

Pape et al. note additional problems in the ways that course completion is defined:

> When does the measure begin? How is completion defined? Do students have a "no penalty" period of enrollment in the online course during which they

> may drop from the course and will not be considered when calculating the course completion rate? Is completion defined as a grade of 60 or 65? How are students who withdrew from the course after the "no penalty" period counted, especially if they withdrew with a passing grade?[5]

Following the recommendations of their evaluators, dLC staff made efforts to communicate definitions of course completion and withdrawal that were internally consistent and made sure each vendor was reporting accurate data based on these conversations. the result was a higher level of consistency and accuracy in data reporting.

There is growing attention to the problem of undefined outcome measures in the field of evaluating online learning. A 2004 report by Cathy Cavanaugh et al., specifically recommended that standards be developed "for reporting the academic and programmatic outcomes of distance learning programs."[6] A nACOL effort is under way to develop benchmarks for measuring program effectiveness and overall standards for program quality. Meanwhile, the best evaluators can do is to ensure internal consistency in the outcome measures used across all of their own data sources. Although the research base is limited, evaluators may be able to find similar studies for ideas on how to define outcomes. Moving forward, online program evaluators can proactively find ways to share research methods and definitions and reach a consensus on the best ways to measure program effectiveness.

Work Collaboratively to Develop New Evaluation Tools

In the early years of Appleton eSchool, school leaders became aware that they needed an overall evaluation system to determine the school's strengths and weaknesses. After failing to find an existing comprehensive tool that would fit their needs, Ben vogel, Appleton's principal and Governance Board chair, and Connie Radtke, Appleton's program leader, began to develop their own evaluation process. their goal was to design an instrument that would identify the core components necessary for students to be successful in an online program. In addition, they wanted to create a process that could be used to prompt dialogue among program leaders, staff, governance board members, and external colleagues, about the components of a successful online learning experience, in order to provide direction for future growth and enhancement.

Through extensive internal discussions and consultation with external colleagues, includ- ing staff from such online programs as virtual High School and Florida virtual School, vogel and Radtke identified eight key program components and developed a rubric for measuring them called the Online Program Perceiver Instrument (OPPI). (See Key Components of Appleton eSchool's Online Program Perceiver Instrument, p. 16.) vogel says, "[Our goal was] to figure out those universal core components that are necessary in a K–12 online program to allow students to be successful... . We were able to share [our initial thoughts] with other people in the K–12 realm, and say, 'What are we missing? And what other pieces should we add?' It just kind of developed from there."

The core components identified in the OPPI are what Appleton leaders see as the essential building blocks for supporting students in an online environment. the eight components address the online program user's entire experience, from first learning about the course or program to completing it.

When developing the OPPI, vogel and Radtke researched many existing online program evaluations in higher education, but found them i nsufficient for building a comprehensive rubric at the K–12 level. vogel notes, for example, that having face-to-face mentors or coaches for students taking online courses is critical at the K–1 2 level, whereas it is not considered so important for older students who are studying online in higher education. to capture this program element, vogel and Radtke included "Program Support" as a key component in the OPPI rubric, focusing on the training given to mentors (usually parents in the Appleton eSchool model) as well as training for local school contacts who support and coordinate local student access to online courses (see table 2, Excerpt from Appleton eSchool's Online Program Perceiver Instrument, p. 17). to assess mentor perception of program quality, the evaluators surveyed them following the completion of each online course.

As part of the OPPI process, vogel and Radtke developed a three-phase approach to internal evaluation, which they refer to as a "self-discovery" process. In the Discovery Phase, program personnel fill out a report that describes the school's practices in each of the eight areas identified in the OPPI. then program decision-makers use the rubric to determine what level of program performance is being attained for each element: deficient, developing, proficient, or exemplary. In addition, program leaders e-mail surveys to students, mentors (usually parents), and teachers at the end of each course, giving them an opportunity to comment on the program's performance in each of the eight OPPI areas. In the Outcome Phase, results from the Discovery Phase report and surveys are summarized, generating a numerical rating in each program area. At the same time, information on student outcomes is reviewed, including student grades, grade point averages, and course completion rates. Program decision-makers synthesize all of this data in an outcome sheet and use it to set goals for future growth and development. Finally, in the Sharing of Best Practices Phase, program leaders may select particular practices to share with other programs. Appleton has partnered with other online programs to form the Wisconsin eSchool network, a consortium of virtual schools that share resources. the network's Web site includes a Best Practices Portfolio and schools using the OPPI are invited to submit examples from their evaluations.[7] Practices that are determined to be in the "proficient" or "exemplary" range are considered for placement in the portfolio, and participating schools are cited for their contributions. the entire evaluation system is Web-based, allowing for streamlined data collection, analysis, and sharing.

Key Components of Appleton eSchool's Online Program Perceiver Instrument (OPPI)

Practitioners and program administrators use the OPPI to evaluate program performance in eight different areas:

1. Program Information: System provides and updates information necessary for prospective users to understand the program being offered and determine whether it may be a good fit for students.
2. Program Orientation: System provides an introduction or orientation that prepares students to be successful in the online course.
3. Program Technology: System provides and supports program users' hardware and software needs in the online environment.
4. Program Curriculum: System provides and supports an interactive curriculum for the online course.
5. Program Teaching: System provides and supports teaching personnel dedicated to online learning and their online students.
6. Characteristics and Skills Displayed by Successful Online Students: System identifies and provides opportunities for students to practice characteristics necessary for success in an online environment.
7. Program Support: System provides and supports a system of support for all online students and mentors (e.g., parents) and coaches.
8. Program Data Collection: System collects data and uses that data to inform program decision-makers and share information with other programs.

Appleton's decision to develop its own evaluation rubric and process provides several advantages. Besides resulting in a perfectly tailored evaluation process, Appleton leaders also have the ability to evaluate their program at any time without waiting for funding or relying on a third-party evaluator. Still, developing an evaluation process is typically expensive and may not be a practical option for many programs. Appleton's leaders spent many hours researching and developing outcome measures (i.e., the descriptions of practice for each program component under each level of program performance). they also invested about $15,000 of their program grant funds to pay a Web developer to design the online system for compiling and displaying evaluation data. For others attempting to develop this type of tailored rubric and process, accessing outside expertise is critical to fill gaps in knowledge or capacity. Appleton leaders collaborated extensively with experienced colleagues from other virtual schools, particularly as they were developing their rubric.

SHARE EVALUATION FINDINGS WITH OTHER PROGRAMS AND EVALUATORS

Although the OPPI rubric was developed specifically for Appleton, from the beginning vogel and Radtke intended to share it with other programs.

This rubric is currently accessible free of charge through the Web site of the Wisconsin eSchool network, described above.[8] vogel explains that the OPPI and its umbrella evaluation system are readily adaptable to other programs: "Internally, this system doesn't ask people to have an overwhelming amount of knowledge. It allows people to make tweaks as needed for their particular programs, but they don't have to create the whole wheel over again [by designing their own evaluation system]." the OPPI system also allows for aggregation of results across multiple programs—a mechanism that would allow groups of schools in a state, for example, to analyze their combined data. to assist schools using the OPPI for the first time, Appleton offers consultation services to teach other users how to interpret and communicate key findings. through their efforts to share their evaluation tool and create the online forum, Appleton leaders have developed an efficient and innovative way to build the knowledge base on online learning programs.

Table 2. Excerpt From Appleton eSchool's Online Program Perceiver Instrument[9]

Component 7. Program Support. the purpose of the support network is to provide additional support to the student that complements the instructor. this includes not only a support person from home, but also other school resources that may include a counselor, social worker, etc.

Element	Level of Program Performance			
	Deficient	Developing	Proficient	Exemplary
Overall Student Support Structure Plan	No student support structure plan in place or the plan is poorly written and/or incom- plete. Students are not receiving necessary resources.	Student support struc- ture plan is in place but parts of the plan are incomplete or may be unclear. The plan provides for resources necessary for student success but some gaps in the plan may exist.	Student support structure plan is in place and is clear in its purpose and objectives. The plan provides for resources necessary for student success.	Exemplary student sup- port structure plan is in place and is a proven model for assuring stu- dents have necessary support and ongoing support.
Mentor responsibi lities have been developed and shared	Mentor responsibilities have not been devel- oped or are incomplete and/or unclear or have not been appropriately shared.	Mentor responsibilities have been developed and shared but parts may be unclear and/ or all mentors have not received the information.	Mentor responsibilities are well written, clear, and have been shared with all mentors.	Mentor responsibilities are extremely well writ- ten, clear, and shared in numerous formats with all mentors.
Mentors are provided necessary training and	No mentor training pro- gram provided or there are no written objectives that	Mentor training program is provided and there are written objectives that	Mentor training program is provided and there are objectives that out- line the	Mentor training program is provided and there are extremely clear and concise

support	clearly outline the purpose of the men- tor training program. No ongoing support is available.	outline the purpose of the mentor training. Some objectives may be unclear. Ongoing support is available, but may be inconsistent.	purpose of the mentor training. Few objectives are unclear. Ongoing support is available.	objectives that outline the purpose of the mentor training pro- gram. Ongoing support is consistently provided.
Mentors provide positive support for student	No system in place to monitor mentor support and/or concerns that may arise.	System in place to monitor mentor support and/or concerns that may arise, but system may break down from time to time.	System in place to mon- itor mentor support and/ or concerns that may arise. System is reliable most of the time.	Proven system in place to monitor mentor sup- port and/or concerns that may arise. The system provides op- portunities for two-way communication.
Mentors have the abil- ity to communicate with teacher	No system in place to allow mentors to com- municate with teacher in a timely manner.	System in place to allow mentors to com- municate with teacher in a timely manner but system may break down from time to time.	System in place to allow mentors to communi- cate with teacher in a timely manner. System is reliable most of the time.	Proven system in place to allow men- tors to communicate with teacher in a timely manner. The system provides check- ins with teacher on a regular basis.

In Louisiana, evaluators from Education Development Center (EDC) have used more conventional channels for sharing findings from the evaluation of the state's Algebra I Online program. this program was created by the Louisiana Department of Education to address the state's shortage of highly qualified algebra teachers, especially in urban and rural settings. In addition, districts desiring to provide certified teachers access to pedagogy training and mentoring so they can build capacity for strong mathematics instruction are eligible to participate. In Algebra I Online courses, students physically attend class in a standard bricks-and-mortar classroom at their home school, which is managed by a teacher who may not be certified to deliver algebra instruction. But once in this classroom, each student has his or her own computer and participates in an online class delivered by a highly qualified (i.e., certified) algebra teacher. the in-class teacher gives students face-to-face assistance, oversees lab activities, proctors tests, and is generally responsible for maintaining an atmosphere that is conducive to learning. the online teacher delivers the algebra instruction, answers students' questions via an online discussion board, grades assignments via e-mail, provides students with feedback on homework and tests, and submits grades. the online and in-class teachers communicate frequently with each other to discuss students' progress and collaborate on how to help students learn the particular content being covered. this interaction between teachers not only benefits students; it also serves as a form of professional development for the in-class instructors. In addition to providing all students with high-quality algebra instruction, a secondary goal of the program is to increase the instructional skills of the in- class teachers and support them in earning their mathematics teaching certificate.

Although its founders believed that the Algebra I Online model offered great promise for addressing Louisiana's shortage of mathematics teachers, when the program was launched in 2002 they had no evidence to back up this belief. the key question was whether such a program could provide students with learning opportunities that were as effective as those in traditional settings. If it were as effective, the program could provide a timely and cost- effective solution for the mathematics teacher shortage. Louisiana needed hard evidence to show whether the program was credible.

Following a number of internal evaluation activities during the program's first two years, in 2004 the program's leaders engaged an external evaluation team consisting of Rebecca Carey of EDC, an organization with experience in researching online learning; Laura O'Dwyer of Boston College's Lynch School of Education; and Glenn Kleiman of the Friday Institute for Educational Innovation at north Carolina State university, College of Education. the evaluators were impressed by the program leaders' willingness to undergo a rigorous evaluation. "We didn't have to do a lot of convincing," says EDC's Carey. "they wanted it to be as rigorous as possible, which was great and, I think, a little bit unusual." the program also was given a boost in the form of a grant from the north Central Regional Educational Laboratory (nCREL), a federally funded education laboratory. the grant funded primary research on the effectiveness of online learning and provided the project with $75,000 beyond its initial $35,000 evaluation budget from the state legislature. the additional funding allowed EDC to add focus groups and in-class observations, as well as to augment its own evaluation capacity by hiring an external consultant with extensive expertise in research methodology and analysis.

The EDC evaluators chose a quasi-experimental design (see Glossary of Common Evaluation terms, p. 65) to compare students enrolled in the online algebra program with those studying algebra only in a traditional face-to-face classroom format. to examine the impact of the Algebra I Online course, they used hierarchical linear modeling to analyze posttest scores and other data collected from the treatment and control groups. to determine if students in online learning programs engaged in different types of peerto-peer interactions and if they perceived their

Learning experiences differently than students in traditional classrooms, the evaluators surveyed students in both environments and conducted observations in half of the treatment classrooms. In total, the evaluators studied Algebra I Online courses and face-to-face courses in six districts.

After completing their assessment, the evaluators produced final reports for the Louisiana Department of Education and nCREL and later wrote two articles about the program for professional journals. the first article, published in the *Journal of Research on Technology in Education*,[10] described Algebra I Online as a viable model for providing effective algebra instruction. In the study, online students showed comparable (and sometimes stronger) test scores, stayed on task, and spent more time interacting with classmates about math content than students in traditional classroom settings. the evaluators speculated that this was a result of the program's unique model, which brings the online students together with their peers at a regularly scheduled time. the evaluators found a few areas for concern as well. For example, a higher percentage of online students reported that they did not have a good learning experience, a finding that is both supported and contradicted by research studies on online learning from higher education. the evaluation also found that the Algebra I Online students felt less confident in their algebra skills than did traditional students, a finding the evaluators feel is particularly ripe for further research efforts. (For additional discussion, see Interpreting the Impact of Program Maturity, p. 40.)

The Algebra I Online evaluators wrote and published a second article in the *Journal of Asynchronous Technologies* that focused on the program as a professional development model for uncertified or inexperienced math teachers.[11] In this piece, the evaluators described the programs' pairing of online and in-class teachers as a "viable online model for providing [the in-class] teachers with an effective model for authentic and embedded professional development that is relevant to their classroom experiences."

Of course, not all programs will have the resources to contribute to the research literature in this manner. In Louisiana's case, the evaluators had extensive expertise in online evaluation and took the time and initiative required for publishing their findings in academic journals. In so doing, they served two purposes: providing the program leaders with the evidence they needed to confidently proceed with Algebra I Online and publishing much-needed research to states that might be considering similar approaches.

SUMMARY

The literature on K–12 online learning is growing. Several publications and resources document emerging best practices and policies in online learning (see appendix A). For program leaders and evaluators who are developing an evaluation, the quality standards from SREB and nACOL provide a basic framework for looking at the quality of online courses and teachers. there also is a growing body of studies from which evaluators can draw lessons and adapt methods; evaluators need not reinvent the wheel. At the same time, they must exercise caution when applying findings, assumptions, or methods from other studies, as online programs and resources vary tremendously in whom they serve, what they offer, and how they offer it. What works best for one program evaluation may not be appropriate for another.

Given the lack of commonly used outcome measures for online learning evaluations, individual programs should at least strive for internal consistency, as dLC has. If working with multiple vendors or school sites, online program leaders need to articulate a clear set of business rules for what data are to be collected and how, distributing these guidelines to all parties who are collecting information. Looking ahead, without these common guidelines, evaluators will be hard pressed to compare their program's outcomes with others. Some of the evaluators featured in this guide have made contributions to the field of online learning evaluation, like Appleton's leaders, who developed an evaluation model that can be borrowed or adapted by other programs, and the evaluators of Algebra I Online, who published their study findings in professional journals.

In: Evaluating Online Learning
Editor: Arthur T. Weston, pp. 35-42
ISBN 978-1-60741-107-9

Chapter 3

EVALUATING MULTIFACETED ONLINE RESOURCES

Like many traditional education programs, online learning resources sometimes offer participants a wide range of learning experiences. their multifaceted offerings are a boon for students or teachers with diverse interests, but can be a dilemma for evaluators seeking uniform findings about effectiveness. In the case of an educational Web site like Washington's dLC, for example, different types of users will explore different resources; some students may take an online course while others may be researching colleges or seeking a mentor. virtual schools that use multiple course providers present a similar conundrum, and even the same online course may offer differentiated learning experiences if, for example, students initiate more or less contact with the course instructor or receive varying degrees of face-to-face support from a parent or coach. (A similar lack of uniformity can be found in traditional settings with different instructors using varying instructional models.)

When faced with a multifaceted resource, how is an evaluator to understand and document the online learning experience, much less determine what value it adds?

Several of the evaluations featured in this guide encountered this issue, albeit in distinct ways. DLC evaluators were challenged to assess how students experienced and benefited from the Web site's broad range of resources. Evaluators of Maryland Public television's thinkport Web site, with its extensive teacher and student resources from many providers, similarly struggled to assess its impact on student achievement. In a very different example, the evaluators for the Arizona virtual Academy (AZvA) faced the challenge of evaluating a hybrid course that included both online and face-to-face components and in which students' individual experiences varied considerably.

COMBINE BREADTH AND DEPTH TO EVALUATE RESOURCE-RICH WEB SITES

With its wide range of services and resources for students and teachers, DLC is a sprawling, diverse project to evaluate. through this centrally hosted Web site, students can access over 300 online courses, including all core subjects and various electives, plus Advanced Placement (AP) and English as a Second Language courses. DLC also offers students online mentors, college and career planning resources, and an extensive digital library. In addition, DLC offers other resources and tools for teachers, including online curricula, activities, and diagnostics. For schools that sign up to use DLC, the program provides training for school personnel to assist them in implementing the Web site's resources.

Initially, DLC's evaluation strategy was to collect broad information about how the Web site is used. Later, program leaders shifted their strategy to focus on fewer and narrower topics that could substantiate the program's efficacy. the evaluators focused on student achievement in the online courses and on school-level supports for educators to help them make the most of DLC's resources. together, the series of DLC evaluations—there have been at least five distinct efforts to date—combine breadth and depth, have built on each other's findings from year to year, and have produced important formative and summative findings (see Glossary of Common Evaluation terms, p. 65).

In the project's first year, Debra Friedman, a lead administrator at the university of Washington (a DLC partner organization), conducted an evaluation that sought information on whom DLC serves and what school conditions and policies best support its use. to answer these questions, the evaluators selected methods designed to elicit information directly from participants, including discussions with DLC administrators, board members, school leaders, and teachers, as well as student and teacher surveys that asked about their use of computers and the Internet and about the utility of the DLC training. the evaluator also looked at a few indicators of student achievement, such as the grades that students received for DLC online courses.

The evaluation yielded broad findings about operational issues and noted the need for DLC to prioritize among its many purposes and audiences. It also uncovered an important finding about student achievement in the online courses:

the greatest percentage of students (52 percent) received Fs, but the next greatest percentage (37 percent) received As. to explain these outcomes, the evaluator pointed to the lack of uniformity in students' motivation and needs, and the type of academic support available to them. the evaluator also noted the varying quality of the vendors who provided courses, finding that "some vendors are flexible and responsive to students' needs; others are notably inflexible. Some are highly professional operations, others less so."[12] this evaluation also described substantial variation in how well schools were able to support the use of dLC resources. the findings helped program administrators who, in response, stepped up their efforts to train educators about the Web portal's resources and how to use it with students. the evaluation also was a jumping-off point for future assessments that would follow up on the themes of student achievement in the online courses and supports for educators to help them take advantage of dLC's offerings.

In the project's second year, project leaders launched another evaluation. this effort consisted of student focus groups to identify students' expectations of dLC's online courses, student pre-course preparation, overall experience, and suggestions for improving the courses and providing better support. As a separate effort, they also contracted with an independent evaluator, Cohen Research and Evaluation, to learn more about the behavior and motivations of students and other users, such as school librarians, teachers, and administrators. this aspect of the evaluation consisted of online surveys with students, teachers, and school librarians; and interviews with selected teachers, librarians, and administrators (primarily to help develop survey questions). to gain insight into how well students were performing in the classes, the evaluators analyzed grades and completion rates for students enrolled in dLC courses. the evaluation activities conducted in the second year again pointed to the need for more school-level support for using dLC resources. the evaluators found that some schools were excited and committed to using the Web site's resources, but were underutilizing it because they lacked sufficient structures, such as training and time for teachers to learn about its offerings, internal communication mechanisms to track student progress, and adequate technical support.

When dLC's leaders began to contemplate a third-year evaluation, they wanted more than basic outcome data, such as student grades and completion rates. "We can count how many courses, we know the favorite subjects, and we know the grade averages and all of that," says Judy Margrath-Huge, dLC president and chief executive officer. What they needed, she explains, was to get at the "so what," meaning they wanted to understand "what difference [dLC] makes."

The evaluation team knew that if its effort were to produce reliable information about dLC's influence on student achievement, it would need to zero in on one, or just a few, of the Web site's many components. Some features—dLC's vast digital library, for example—simply were not good candidates for the kind of study they planned to conduct. As Karl nelson, dLC's director of technology and operations, explains, "It is very difficult to evaluate the effectiveness of and to answer a 'so what' question about a library database, for example. It's just hard to point to a kid using a library database and then a test score going up." ultimately, says nelson, dLC's leaders chose to look primarily at the online courses, believing that this was the feature they could best evaluate.

DLC leaders hired outside evaluators, Fouts & associates, to help them drill down into a specific aspect of student achievement—determining the role that dLC online courses play in: 1) enabling students to graduate from high school and 2) helping students become eligible and fully prepared for college. In this evaluation, the researchers identified a sample of 115 graduated seniors from 17 schools who had completed dLC courses. the evaluators visited the schools to better understand online course-taking policies and graduation requirements and to identify dLC courses on the transcripts of these 115 students. at the school sites, evaluators interviewed school coordinators and examined student achievement data, student transcripts, and dLC documents.

The evaluation gave dLC's leaders what they wanted: concrete evidence of the impact of dLC online courses. this study showed that 76 percent of students who took an online course through dLC did so because the class was not available at their school and that one-third of the students in the study would not have graduated without the credits from their online course. this and other evaluation findings, show that "we are meeting our mission," says Margrath-Huge. "We are accomplishing what we were set out to accomplish. and it's really important for us to be able to stand and deliver those kinds of messages with that kind of data behind us." dLC has used its evaluation findings in multiple ways, including when marketing the program to outsiders, to demonstrate its range of offerings and its effect on students (see fig. 1, Excerpt from digital

Learning Commons' *Meeting 21st Century Learning Challenges in Washington State*, p. 24).

It would be impossible to conduct a comprehensive evaluation of everything that dLC has to offer, but certainly the evaluation strategy of combining breadth and depth has given it a great deal of useful information. dLC's leaders have used the findings from all the evaluations to improve their offerings and to demonstrate effectiveness to funders and other stakeholders.

In Maryland, thinkport evaluators faced a similar challenge in trying to study a vast Web site that compiles educational resources for teachers and students. at first, the evaluation team from Macro International, a research, management, and information technology firm, conducted such activities as gathering satisfaction data, reviewing Web site content, and documenting how the site was used. But over time, project leaders were asked by funders to provide more concrete evidence about thinkport's impact on student performance. the evaluation (and the project itself) had to evolve to meet this demand.

In response, the team decided to "retrofit" the evaluation in 2005, settling on a two-part evaluation that would offer both breadth and depth. First, the evaluators surveyed all registered users about site usage and satisfaction, and second, they designed a randomized controlled trial (see Glossary of Common Evaluation terms, p. 65) to study how one of the site's most popular features—an "electronic field trip"—affected students' learning. Several field trips had been developed under this grant; the one selected was Pathways to Freedom, about slavery and the underground Railroad. this particular product was chosen for a number of reasons: most middle school social studies curricula include the topic; the evaluators had observed the field trip in classrooms in an earlier formative study and were aware of students' high interest in its topics and activities; and Web site statistics indicated that it was a heavily viewed and utilized resource.

The evaluators gave pre- and posttests of content knowledge about slavery and the underground Railroad to students whose teachers used the electronic field trip and control groups of students whose teachers used traditional instruction. they found that the electronic field trip had a very substantial positive impact on student learning, particularly among students whose teachers had previously used it: these students of experienced teachers scored 121 percent higher on the content knowledge test than the students whose teachers used traditional instruction.

Like the dLC evaluation, the thinkport evaluation proved useful both for formative and summative purposes. thinkport's leaders learned that teachers who were new to the electronic field trip needed more training and experience to successfully incorporate it into their classrooms. they also learned that once teachers knew how to use the tool, their students learned the unit's content far better than their peers in traditional classes. the evaluators' two-part plan gave thinkport's leaders what they needed: broad information about usage and satisfaction and credible evidence that a frequently used feature has a real impact on students.

Independent research demonstrates increased on-time graduation rates and college/workforce readiness.

The results are clear—DLC access to online courses increases on-time graduation rates at schools studied in Washington State.

When online courses are made available through the DLC to students who would not otherwise have had access to that course—whether for purposes of remediation, advanced placement, or college entrance—it makes a significant difference, increasing graduation rates and college/workforce readiness.

Research focused on online courses

The DLC has focused their evaluation research on the impact from online courses, as outcomes and results can be objectively gathered and tabulated. Over two years worth of data demonstrate consistent results.

2006 Evaluation Results

In the spring of 2006 researchers from Fouts & Associates analyzed the transcripts of approximately 115 students at seventeen DLC-participating high schools across the state. Quantitative and qualitative data were gathered from transcripts, student achievement data, DLC documents, and school coordinators to identify whether access to online courses through the DLC could objectively be shown to make a difference.

Online Course Registrations

When the DLC was launched, online course enrollment was projected to reach 200 students. During the 2004-05 school year alone, however, 1,159 students from forty-two high schools took an online course. So, what courses are students taking online? Our data indicate significant growth in foreign languages over the last year. Our 2004-05 statistics on enrollment in advanced coursework are consistent with those of NCES, which reports that 14% of enrollments nationally are in AP or college-level courses.

1. INCREASED GRADUATION RATES: Of the 115 students who graduated, approximately 33% would NOT have graduated without a course made available through the DLC.

2. COLLEGE AND WORKFORCE READINESS: Of the fifty-nine students who were college eligible, thirty-six students – 61% – took advanced classes to better prepare themselves for college.

The Digital Learning Commons | Meeting 21st Century Learning Challenges in Washington State 3

Figure 1. Excerpt From Digital Learning Commons' Meeting 21st Century Learning Challenges in Washington State.[13]

USE MULTIPLE METHODS TO CAPTURE WIDE-RANGING STUDENT EXPERIENCES IN ONLINE COURSES

In the examples above, evaluators struggled to wrap their arms around sprawling Web resourc- es that lacked uniformity. Sometimes a similar challenge is found at the micro level, as when students have heterogeneous experiences in the same online class. the leaders of Arizona's AZvA struggled with this problem when they set out to evaluate one of their online courses.

In 2006, AZvA school leaders began to experiment with hybrid courses—regular online classes supplemented with weekly face-to-face lessons from a classroom teacher. the in-person component was originally designed in a very structured way: Students received classroom instruction every week at a specific time and location, and they had to commit to this weekly instruction for an entire semester. In addition, students could participate in the hybrid class only if they were working either on grade level or no more than one level below grade level. these restrictions allowed the face-to-face teachers to offer the same lessons to all students during the weekly session. School leaders specifically designed this structure to bring uniformity to students' experiences and make it easier to evaluate the class. As AZvA's director, Mary Gifford, explains, "We wanted the hybrid experience to be the same for all the kids so we could actually determine whether or not it is increasing student achievement."

However, when program leaders surveyed parents at the semester break, Gifford says, "Parents offered some very specific feedback." they didn't like the semester-long, once-a-week commitment, and they argued that the structure prevented students from working at their own pace. Instead, parents wanted a drop-in model that would offer students more flexibility and tailored assistance. In response, she says, "We totally overhauled the course for the second semester and made it a different kind of a model."

In the new format, teachers do not deliver prepared lessons, but, instead, work with students one-on-one or in small groups on any topic with which a student is struggling.

While the flexibility of the new model meets student needs, students naturally will have more varied experiences using it and school leaders will not be able to isolate its effect on student achievement. In other words, observed gains could be due to any number of factors, such as how frequently the student drops in, whether a student works one-on-one with a teacher or in a small group, and what content is covered during the drop-in session. In this instance, the needs of program participants necessarily outweighed those of the evaluation.

However, because the school has a number of other data collection efforts in place, Gifford and her colleagues will still be able to gather information about whether the hybrid model is helping students. School administrators track how frequently students attend the drop-in class and chart students' academic progress through the curriculum both before and after they participate in the hybrid program. aZva also separately examines state test scores for students who attend the hybrid program on a regular basis. In addition, aZva frequently uses surveys of parents, students, and teachers to gather information about the effectiveness of many aspects of their program, including the hybrid class. these kinds of activities can provide important insights when controlled studies are impossible.

SUMMARY

Though multifaceted resources can make it difficult for evaluators to gauge effectiveness, good evaluations—especially those using multiple, complementary research methods—can identify the circumstances under which the program or resource is most likely to succeed or fail and can generate useful recommendations for strengthening weak points. Evaluators who are studying multifaceted resources should consider a strategy that combines both breadth and depth.

If studying an educational Web site that offers an array of resources, evaluators might collect broad information about site usage and then select one or two particular features to examine in more depth. Program leaders can facilitate this process by clearly articulating what each resource is intended to do, or what outcomes they would hope to see if the resource was being used effectively. From this list, program leaders and evaluators can work together to determine what to study and how. In some instances, it might be logical to design a multiyear evaluation that focuses on distinct program components in different years, or collects broad information in the first year, and narrows in focus in subsequent years.

If evaluating a particular course or resource that offers students a wide range of experiences, evaluators might consider using a mix of quantitative and qualitative methods to provide a well- rounded assessment of it. Rich, descriptive information about students' experiences with the course or resource can be useful when trying to interpret data about student outcomes.

In: Evaluating Online Learning
Editor: Arthur T. Weston, pp. 43-52
ISBN 978-1-60741-107-9

Chapter 4

FINDING APPROPRIATE COMPARISON GROUPS

When evaluators have research questions about an online program's impact on student achieve- ment, their best strategy for answering those questions is often an experimental design, like a randomized controlled trial, or a quasi-experimental design that requires them to find matched comparison groups. these two designs are the best, most widely accepted methods for determining program effects (see table 3, p. 28).

Evaluators who use these methods must proceed carefully. they must first ensure that comparisons are appropriate, taking into consideration the population served and the program's goals and structure. For example, online programs dedicated to credit recovery[14] would want to compare their student outcomes with those of other credit recovery programs because they are serving similiar populations. Evaluators must also be scrupulous in their efforts to find good comparison groups—often a challenging task. For a particular online class, there may be no corresponding face-to-face class. Or it may be difficult to avoid a self-selection bias if students (or teachers) have chosen to participate in an online program. Or the online program might serve a wide range of students, possibly from multiple states, with a broad range of ages, or with different levels of preparation, making it difficult to compare to a traditional setting or another online program. Evaluators attempting to conduct a randomized controlled trial can encounter an even greater challenge in devising a way to randomly assign students to receive a treatment (see Glossary of Common Evaluation terms, p. 65) online.

How might evaluators work around these comparison group difficulties?

Several of the evaluations featured in this guide sought to compare distance learning programswith face-to-face learning settings, and they took various approaches to the inherent technical challenges of doing so. despite some difficulties along the way, the evaluators of online projects in Louisiana, Alabama, and Maryland all successfully conducted comparative studies that yielded important findings for their programs.

IDENTIFY WELL-MATCHED CONTROL GROUPS FOR QUASI-EXPERIMENTAL STUDIES

In designing the evaluation for Louisiana's Algebra I Online, program leaders in the Louisiana department of Education wanted to address the bottom line they knew policymakers cared about most: whether students in the program's online courses were performing as well as students studying algebra in a traditional classroom.

To implement the quasi-experimental design of their evaluation (see Glossary of Common Evaluation terms, p. 65), the program's administrators needed to identify traditional algebra classrooms to use as controls. the idea was to identify standard algebra courses serving students similar to those participating in the Algebra I Online program and then give pre- and post-course tests to both groups to compare how much each group learned, on average. Of course, in a design such as this, a number of factors besides the class format (online or face-to-face) could affect students' performance: student-level factors, such as individual ability and home environment; teacher-level factors, such as experience and skill in teaching algebra; and school-level factors, such as out-of-class academic supports for students. Clearly, it was important to the evaluation to find the closest matches possible.

Table 3. Evaluation Design Characteristics

Design	Characteristics	Advantage s	Disadvantages
Experime ntal design	Incorporates random assignment of participants to treatment and control groups. The purpose of randomization is to ensure that all possible ex- planations for changes (measured and unmea- surable) in	Most sound or valid study design available Most	Institutional policy guidelines may make random assignment impossible.

	outcomes are taken into account, randomly distributing participants in both the treatment and control groups so there should be no systematic baseline differences. Treatment and control groups are compared on outcome measures. Any differences in outcomes may be assumed to be attributable to the intervention.	accepted in scientific community	
Quasi- experime ntal design	Involves developing a treatment group and a carefully matched comparison group (or groups). Differences in outcomes between the treatment and comparison groups are analyzed, controlling for baseline differences between them on background characteristics and variables of interest.	More practical in most educational settings Widely accepted in scientific community	Finding and choosing suitable treatment and comparison groups can be difficult. Because of nonrandom group assignment, the outcomes of interest in the study may have been influenced not only by the treatment but also by variables not studied.

Source: Adapted from U.S. Department of Education, Mobilizing for Evidence-Based Character Education (2007). Available from http://www.ed.gov/programs /charactered/ mobilizing.pdf

Under a tight timeline, program administrators worked with all their participating districts to identify traditional classrooms that were matched demographically to the online classes and, then, administered a pretest of general mathematics ability to students in both sets of classes. External evaluators from the Education development Center (EdC) joined the effort at this point. although impressed by the work that the program staff had accomplished given time and budget constraints, the EdC evaluators were concerned about the quality of matches between the treatment and control classes. Finding good matches is a difficult task under the best of circumstances and, in this case, it proved even more difficult for non- evaluators, that is, program and school administrators. The quality of the matches was especially problematic in small districts or nonpublic schools that had fewer control classrooms from which to choose. EdC evaluator Rebecca Carey says, “To their credit, [the program’s administrators] did the best they could in the amount of time they had.” Still, she adds, “the matches weren’t necessarily that great across the control and the experimental. ... Had we been involved from the beginning, we might have been a little bit more stringent about how the control schools would match to the intervention schools and, maybe, have made the selection process a little bit more rigorous.”

Ultimately, the evaluation team used students’ pretest scores to gauge whether the treatment and control group students started the course with comparable skills and knowledge and employed advanced statistical techniques to help control for some of the poor matches.

In their report, the evaluators also provided data on differences between the control and treatment groups (e.g., student characteristics, state test scores in math, size of the school), and they drew from other data sources (including surveys and observations) to triangulate their findings (see Common Problems When Comparing Online Programs to Face-to-Face Programs, p. 30). to other programs considering a comparative study, the Algebra I Online evaluators recommend involving the evaluation team early in the planning process and having them supervise the matching of treatment and control groups.

The evaluators of Alabama’s Alabama Connecting Classrooms, Educators, & Students Statewide Distance Learning (ACCESS) initiative similarly planned a quasi-experimental design and needed traditional classes to use as matches. ACCESS provides a wide range of distance courses, including core courses, electives, remedial courses, and advanced courses, which are either Web-based, utilize interactive videoconferencing (IvC) platforms, or use a combination of both technologies. In the case of IvC courses, distance learners receive instruction from a teacher who is delivering a face-to-face class at one location while the distance learners participate from afar.

When external evaluators set out to compare the achievement of ACCESS’s IvC students to that of students in traditional classrooms, they decided to take advantage of the program’s distinctive format. As controls, they used the classrooms where the instruction was delivered live by the same instructor. In other words, the students at the site receiving the IvC feed were considered the treatment group, and students at the sending site were the control group. this design helped evaluators to isolate the effect of the class format (IvC or face-to-face) and to avoid capturing the effects of differences in style and skill among teachers, a problem they would have had if the treatment and control classes were taught by different people. Martha Donaldson, ACCESS's lead program administrator, says, "We were looking to see if it makes a difference whether students are face-to-face with the teacher or if they're receiving instruction in another part of the state via the distance learning equipment." to compare performance between the two groups of students, evaluators gathered a range of data, including grades, scores on Advanced Placement tests, if relevant, and enrollment and dropout data. the design had some added logistical benefits for the evaluators: it was easier to have the control classrooms come from schools participating in ACCESS, rather than having to collect data from people who were unfamiliar with the program.

Common Problems When Comparing Online Programs to Faceto-Face Programs

Evaluators need to consider both student- and school- or classroom-level variables when they compare online and face-to-face programs. At the student level, many online program participants enroll because of a particular circumstance or attribute, and thus they cannot be randomly assigned—for example, a student who takes an online course over the summer to catch up on credits. The inherent selection bias makes it problematic to compare the results of online and face-to-face students. Evaluators' best response is to find, wherever possible, control groups that are matched as closely as possible to the treatment groups; this includes matching for student demographic characteristics; their reason for taking the course (e.g., credit recovery); and their achievement level. Classroom- and school-level factors complicate comparisons as well. If the online program is more prevalent in certain types of schools (e.g., rural schools) or classrooms (e.g., those lacking a fully certified teacher), then the comparison unintentionally can capture the effects of these differences. Evaluators need to understand and account for these factors when selecting control groups.

Despite these benefits, the strategy of using IvC sending sites as control groups did have a few drawbacks. For instance, the evaluators were not able to match treatment and control groups on characteristics that might be important, such as student- and school-level factors. It is possible that students in the receiving sites attended schools with fewer resources, for example, and the comparison had no way to control for that. For these reasons, the ACCESS evaluators ultimately chose not to repeat the comparison between IvC sending and receiving sites the following year. they did, however, suggest that such a comparison could be strengthened by collecting data that gives some indication of students' pretreatment ability level—GPA, for example—and using statistical techniques to control for differences. Another strategy, they propose, might be to limit the study to such a subject area as math or foreign language, where courses follow a sequence and students in the same course (whether online or traditional) would have roughly similar levels of ability.

ANTICIPATE THE CHALLENGES OF CONDUCTING A RANDOMIZED CONTROLLED TRIAL

Evaluators in Maryland had a different challenge on their hands when they were engaged to study thinkport and its wide-ranging education offerings—including lesson plans, student activities, podcasts,[15] video clips, blogs,[16] learning games, and information about how all of these things can be used effectively in classrooms. When asked by a key funder to evaluate the program's impact on student learning, the evaluation team chose to study one of thinkport's most popular features, its collection of "electronic field trips," each one a self-contained curricular unit that includes rich multimedia content (delivered online) and accompanying teacher support materials that assist with standards alignment and lesson planning.

In collaboration with its evaluation partner, Macro International, the program's parent organization, Maryland Public television, set out to study how the Pathways to Freedom electronic field trip impacted student learning in the classroom and whether it added value. Rather than conducting a quasi-experimental study in which the evaluator would have to find control groups that demographically matched existing groups that were receiving a treatment, the thinkport evaluators wanted an experimental design study in which students were assigned randomly to either treatment or control groups.

Although they knew it would require some extra planning and coordination, the evaluators chose to conduct a randomized controlled trial. this design could provide them with the strongest and most reliable measure of the program's effects. But first, there were challenges to overcome. If students in the treatment and control groups were in the same classroom, evaluators thought, they might share information about the field trip and "contaminate" the experiment. Even having treatment and control groups in the same school could cause problems: In addition to the possibility of contamination, the evaluators were concerned that teachers and students in control classrooms would feel cheated by not having access to the field trip and would complain to administrators.

To overcome these challenges and maintain the rigor of the experimental design, program leaders decided to randomize at the school level. They recruited nine schools in two districts and involved all eighth-grade social studies teachers in each school, a total of 23 teachers. The evaluators then matched the schools based on student demographics, teacher data, and student scores on the state assessment. (One small school was coupled with another that matched it demographically, and the two schools were counted as one.) The evaluators then randomly identified one school in each pair as a treatment school and one as a control school. Teachers did not know until training day whether they had been selected as a treatment or control. (The control group teachers were told that they would be given an orientation and would be able to use the electronic field trip after the study.)

A second challenge for the evaluation team was ensuring that teachers in the control classrooms covered the same content as the teachers who were using the electronic field trip—a problem that might also be found in quasi-experimental designs that require matched comparison groups. They were concerned because the electronic field trip devotes six class periods to the topic of slavery and the underground Railroad—perhaps more time than is typical in a regular classroom. To ensure that students in both groups would spend a similar amount of time on the underground Railroad unit and have varied resources to use, the evaluators provided additional curricular materials to the control teachers, including books, dvds, and other supplemental materials. On each of the six days they delivered the unit, all teachers in the study completed forms to identify the standards they were covering, and they also completed a form at the end of the study to provide general information about their lessons. during the course of the unit, the evaluators found that the control teachers began working together to pool their resources and develop lesson plans. The evaluators did not discourage this interaction, believing that it increased the control teachers' ability to deliver the content effectively and, ultimately, added credibility to the study. To compare how well students learned the content of the unit, the evaluators assessed students' knowledge of slavery and the underground Railroad before and after the instructional unit was delivered.

The evaluators' approach to these challenges was thoughtful and effective. By balancing the experimental design concept with practical considerations, the evaluation team was able to get the information they wanted and successfully complete the study.

SUMMARY

The evaluations of Algebra I Online, ACCESS, and Thinkport illustrate a variety of approaches to constructing comparative studies. For program leaders who are considering an evaluation that will compare the performance of online and traditional students, there are several important considerations. First, program leaders should work with an evaluator to ensure that comparisons are appropriate. together, they will want to take into account the program's goals, the student population served, and the program's structure.

Highlights From the Three Comparative Analyses Featured in this Section

The comparative analyses described in this section produced a number of mportant findings for program staff and leaders to consider.

Algebra I Online (Louisiana). A quasi-experimental study that compared students' performance on a posttest of algebra content knowledge showed that students who participated in the Algebra I Online course performed at least as well as those who participated in the traditional algebra I course, and on average outscored them on 1 8 of the 25 test items. In addition, the data suggested that students in the online program tended to do better than control students on those items that required them to create an algebraic expression from a real-world example. A majority of students in both groups reported having a good or satisfactory learning experience in their algebra course, but online students were more likely to report not having a good experience and were less likely to report feeling confident in their algebra skills. Online students reported spending more time interacting with other students about the math content of the course or working together on course activities than their peers in traditional algebra classrooms; the amount of time they spent socializing, interacting to understand assignment directions, and working together on in-class assignments or homework was about the same. The evaluation also suggested that teacher teams that used small group work and had frequent communication with each other were the most successful.

ACCESS (Alabama). Overall, the evaluations of the program found that ACCESS was succeeding in expanding access to a range of courses and was generally well received by users. The comparative analyses suggested that students taking Advanced Placement (AP) courses from a distance were almost as likely to receive a passing course grade as those students who received instruction in person, and showed that both students and faculty found the educational experience in the distance courses was equal to or better than that of traditional, face-to-face courses. The evaluation also found that in the fall semester of 2006, the distance course dropout rate was significantly lower than nationally reported averages.

Thinkport (Maryland). The randomized controlled trial initially revealed that, compared to traditional instruction, the online field trip did not have a significant positive or negative impact on student learning. However, further analysis revealed that teachers using the electronic field trip for the first time actually had less impact on student learning than those using traditional instruction, while teachers who had used the electronic field trip before had a significantly more positive impact. In a second phase of the study, the evaluators confirmed the importance of experience with the product: when teachers in one district used the electronic field trip again, they were much more successful on their second try, and their students were found to have learned far more than students receiving traditional instruction.

Second, program leaders should clearly articulate the purpose of the comparison. Is the evaluation seeking to find out if the online program is *just as* effective as the traditional one, or *more* effective? In some instances, when online programs are being used to expand access to courses or teachers, for example, a finding of "no significant difference" between online and traditional formats can be acceptable. In these cases, being clear about the purpose of the evaluation ahead of time will help manage stakeholders' expectations.

If considering a quasi-experimental design, evaluators will want to plan carefully for what classes will be used as control groups, and assess the ways they are different from the treatment classes. they will want to consider what kinds of students the class serves, whether the students (or teachers) chose to participate in the treatment or control class, whether students are taking the treatment and control classes for similar reasons (e.g., credit recovery), and whether the students in the treatment and control classes began the class at a similar achievement level. If a randomized controlled trial is desired, evaluators will need to consider how feasible it is for the particular program. Is it possible to randomly assign students either to receive the treatment or be in the control group? Can the control group students receive the treatment at a future date? Will control and treatment students be in the same classroom or school, and if so, might this cause "contamination" of data?

Finally, there are a host of practical considerations if an evaluation will require collecting data from control groups. as we describe further in the next section, program leaders and evaluators need to work together to communicate the importance of the study to anyone who will collect data from control group participants, and to provide appropriate incentives to both the data collectors and the participants. the importance of these tasks can hardly be overstated: the success of a comparative study hinges on having adequate sets of data to compare.

In: Evaluating Online Learning
Editor: Arthur T. Weston, pp. 53-62
ISBN 978-1-60741-107-9

Chapter 5

SOLVING DATA COLLECTION PROBLEMS

Evaluators of any kind of program frequently face resistance to data collection efforts. Surveys or activity logs can be burdensome, and analyzing test scores or grades can seem invasive. In the online arena, there can be additional obstacles. the innovative nature of online programs can sometimes create problems: Some online program administrators simply may be struggling to get teachers or students to use a new technology, let alone respond to a questionnaire about the experience. and in the context of launching a new program or instructional tool, program staffers often have little time to spend on such data collection matters as tracking survey takers or following up with nonrespondents.

Still more difficult is gaining cooperation from people who are disconnected from the program or evaluation—not uncommon when a new high-tech program is launched in a decades-old institution. Other difficulties can arise when online programs serve students in more than one school district or state. Collecting test scores or attendance data, for example, from multiple bureaucracies can impose a formidable burden. Privacy laws present another common hurdle when online evaluators must deal with regulations in multiple jurisdictions to access secondary data. the problem can be compounded when officials are unfamiliar with a new program and do not understand the evaluation goals.

When faced with these data collection challeng- es, how should evaluators respond, and how can they avoid such problems in the first place?

Among the evaluations featured in this guide, data collection problems were common. When study participants did not cooperate with data collection efforts, the evaluators of Chicago Public Schools' virtual High School and Louisiana's algebra I Online program handled the problem by redesigning their evaluations. Thinkport evaluators headed off the same problem by taking proactive steps to ensure cooperation and obtain high data collection rates in their study. When evaluators of Washington's digital Learning Commons (dLC) struggled to collect and aggregate data across multiple private vendors who provided courses through the program, the program took steps to define indicators and improve future evaluation efforts. As these examples show, each of these challenges can be lessened with advance planning and communication. While these steps can be time-consuming and difficult, they are essential for collecting the data needed to improve programs.

Redesign or Refocus the Evaluation when Necessary

In 2004, Chicago Public Schools (CPS) established the virtual High School (CPS/vHS) to provide students with access to a wide range of online courses taught by credentialed teachers. The program seemed like an economical way to meet several district goals: Providing all students with highly qualified teachers; expanding access to a wide range of courses, especially for traditionally underserved students; and addressing the problem of low enrollment in certain high school courses. Concerned about their students' course completion rates, CPS/vHS administrators wanted to learn how to strengthen student preparedness and performance in their program. Seeing student readiness as critical to a successful online learning experience, the project's independent evaluator, TA Consulting, and district administrators focused on student orientation and support; in particular, they wanted to assess the effectiveness of a tutorial tool developed to orient students to online course taking.

At first, evaluators wanted a random selection of students assigned to participate in the orientation tutorial in order to create treatment and control groups (see Glossary of Common Evaluation Terms, p. 65) for an experimental study. While the district approved of the random assignment plan, many school sites were not familiar with the evaluation and did not follow through on getting students to take the tutorial or on tracking who did take it.

To address this problem, the researchers changed course midway through the study, refocusing it on the preparedness of in-class mentors who supported the online courses. This change kept the focus on student support and preparation, but sidestepped the problem of assigning students randomly to the tutorial. In the revised design, evaluators collected data directly from participating students and mentors, gathering information about students' ability to manage time, the amount of on-task time students needed for success, and the level of student and mentor technology skills. The evaluators conducted surveys and focus groups with participants, as well as interviews with the administrators of CPS/vHS and Illinois virtual High School (IvHS), the umbrella organization that provides online courses through CPS/vHS and other districts in the state. They also collected data on student grades and participation in orientation activities. To retain a comparative element in the study, evaluators analyzed online course completion data for the entire state: They found that CPS/vHS course completion rates were 10 to 15 percent lower than comparable rates for all students in IvHS in the fall of 2004 and spring of 2005, but in the fall of 2005, when fewer students enrolled, CPS/vHS showed its highest completion rate ever, at 83.6 percent, surpassing IvHS's informal target of 70 percent.[17]

Through these varied efforts, the researchers were able to get the information they needed. When their planned data collection effort stalled, they went back to their study goals and identified a different indicator for student support and a different means of collecting data on it. And although the experimental study of the student orientation tutorial was abandoned, the evaluators ultimately provided useful information about this tool by observing and reporting on its use to program administrators.

Evaluators very commonly have difficulty collecting data from respondents who do not feel personally invested in the evaluation, and online program evaluators are no exception. In the case of Louisiana's Algebra I Online program, evaluators faced problems getting data from control group teachers. Initially, the state department of education had hoped to conduct a quasi-experimental study (see Glossary of Common Evaluation terms, p. 65) comparing the performance of students in the online program with students in face-to-face settings. Knowing it might be a challenge to find and collect data from control groups across the state, the program administrators required participating districts to agree up front to identify traditional classrooms (with student demographics matching those of online courses) that would participate in the collection of data necessary for ongoing program evaluation. It was a proactive move, but even with this agreement in place, the external evaluator found it difficult to get control teachers to administer posttests at the end of their courses. the control teachers had been identified, but they were far removed from the program and its evaluation, and many had valid concerns about giving up a day of instruction to issue the test. In the end, many of the students in the comparison classrooms did not complete posttests; only about 64 percent of control students were tested compared to 89 percent of online students. In 2005, hurricanes Katrina and Rita created additional problems, as many of the control group classrooms were scattered and data were lost.

In neither the Chicago nor the Louisiana case could the problem of collecting data from unmotivated respondents be tackled head-on, with incentives or redoubled efforts to follow up with nonrespondents, for example. (As is often the case, such efforts were prohibited by the projects' budgets.) Instead, evaluators turned to other, more readily available data. When planning an evaluation, evaluators are wise to try to anticipate likely response rates and patterns and to develop a "Plan B" in case data collection efforts do not go as planned. In some cases, the best approach may be to minimize or eliminate any assessments that are unique to the evaluation and rely instead on existing state or district assessment data that can be collected without burdening students or teachers participating in control groups. the *Federal Education Rights and Privacy Act* (FERPA) allows districts and schools to release student records to a third party for the purpose of evaluations.[18]

Both the Chicago and Louisiana examples serve as cautionary tales for evaluators who plan to undertake an experimental design. If evaluators plan to collect data from those who do not see themselves benefiting from the program or evaluation, the evaluation will need adequate money to provide significant incentives or, at a minimum, to spend substantial time and effort on communication with these individuals.

Take Proactive Steps to Boost Response Rates

In the evaluation of thinkport's electronic field trip, Maryland Public television was more successful in collecting data from control group classrooms. this program's evaluation efforts differed from others in that it did not rely on participation from parties outside of the program. Instead, evaluators first chose participating schools, then assigned them to either a treatment group that participated in the electronic field trip right away or to a control group that could use the lessons in a later semester. teachers in both groups received a one-hour introduction to the study, where they learned about what content they were expected to cover with their students, and about the data collection activities in which they were expected to participate. teachers were informed on that day whether their classroom would be a treatment or control classroom; then control teachers were dismissed, and treatment teachers received an additional two-hour training on how to use the electronic field trip with their students. Control teachers were given the option of receiving the training at the conclusion of the study, so they could use the tool in their classrooms at a future point. as an incentive, the program offered approximately $2,000 to the social studies departments that housed both the treatment and control classes.

Evaluators took other steps that may have paved the way for strong compliance among the control group teachers. they developed enthusiasm for the project at the ground level by first approaching social studies coordinators who became advocates for and facilitators of the project. By approaching these content experts, the evaluators were better able to promote the advantages of participating in the program and its evaluation.

Evaluators reported that coordinators were eager to have their teachers receive training on a new classroom tool, especially given the reputation of Maryland Public television. In turn, the social studies coordinators presented information about the study to social studies teachers during opening meetings and served as contacts for interested teachers. the approach worked: Evaluators were largely able to meet their goal of having all eighth-grade social studies teachers from nine schools participate, rather than having teachers scattered throughout a larger number of schools. Besides having logistical benefits for the evaluators, this accomplishment may have boosted compliance with the study's requirements among participating teachers.

Evaluators also took the time to convince teachers of the importance of the electronic field trip. Before meeting with teachers, evaluators mapped the field trip's academic content to the specific standards of the state and participating schools' counties. they could then say to teachers: "these are the things your students have to do, and this is how the electronic field trip helps them do it." Finally, evaluators spent time explaining the purpose and benefits of the evaluation itself and communicating to teachers that they played an important role in discovering whether a new concept worked.

The overall approach was even more successful than the evaluators anticipated and helped garner commitment among the participating teachers, including those assigned to the control group. the teachers fulfilled the data collection expectations outlined at the onset of the study, including keeping daily reports for the six days of the instructional unit being evaluated and completing forms about the standards that they were teaching, as well as documenting general information about their lessons. By involving control teachers in the experimental process and giving them full access to the treatment, the evaluators could collect the data required to complete the comparative analysis they planned.

Besides facing the challenge of collecting data from control groups, many evaluators, whether of online programs or not, struggle even to collect information from regular program participants. Cognizant of this problem, evaluators are always looking for ways to collect data that are unobtrusive and easy for the respondent to supply. this is an area where online programs can actually present some advantages. For example, Appleton eSchool evaluators have found that online courses offer an ideal opportunity to collect survey data from participants. In some instances, they have required that students complete surveys (or remind their parents to do so) before they can take the final exam for the course. Surveys are e-mailed directly to students or parents, ensuring high response rates and eliminating the need to enter data into a database. Appleton's system keeps individual results anonymous but does allow evaluators to see which individuals have responded.

With the help of its curriculum provider, K12 Inc., the Arizona virtual Academy (AZvA) also frequently uses Web-based surveys to gather feedback from parents or teachers about particular events or trainings they have offered. Surveys are kept short and are e-mailed to respondents immediately after the event. AZvA administrators believe the burden on respondents is relatively minimal, and report that the strategy consistently leads to response rates of about 60 percent. the ease of AZvA's survey strategy encourages program staff to survey frequently. Furthermore, K12 Inc. compiles the results in Microsoft Excel, making them easy for any staff member to read or merge into a PowerPoint presentation (see fig. 2, Example of tabulated Results From an Arizona virtual Academy Online Parent Survey, p. 38). Because the school receives anonymous data from K12 Inc., parents know they may be candid in their comments. With immediate, easyto-understand feedback, AZvA staff are able to fine-tune their program on a regular basis.

Web sites and online courses can offer other opportunities to collect important information with no burden on the participant. For example, evaluators could analyze the different pathways users take as they navigate through a particular online tool or Web site, or how much time is spent on different portions of a Web site or online course. If users are participants in a program and are asked to enter an identifying number when they sign on to the site, this type of information could also be linked to other data on participants, such as school records.

Define Data Elements across Many Sources

Another common problem for online evaluators is the challenge of collecting and aggregating data from multiple sources. As noted earlier, Washington state's dLC offers a wide array of online resources for students and educators. to understand how online courses contribute to students' progress toward a high school diploma and college readiness, the program evaluators conducted site visits to several high schools offering courses through dLC. In reviewing student transcripts, however, the evaluators discovered that schools did not have the same practices for maintaining course completion data and that DLC courses were awarded varying numbers of credits at different schools—the same dLC course might earn a student .5 credit, 1 credit, 1.5 credits, or 2 credits. This lack of consistency made it difficult to aggregate data across sites and to determine the extent to which dLC courses helped students to graduate from high school or complete a college preparation curriculum.

The evaluation final report recommended developing guidelines to show schools how to properly gather student-level data on each participating dLC student in order to help with future evaluations and local assessment of the program's impact.

Plan Ahead When Handling Sensitive Data

Any time evaluators are dealing with student data, there are certain to be concerns about privacy. districts are well aware of this issue, and most have guidelines and data request processes in place to make sure that student data are handled properly. Of course, it is critically important to protect student privacy, but for evaluators, these regulations can create difficulties. For example, in Chicago, Tom Clark, of TA Consulting, had a close partnership with the district's Office of Technology Services, yet still had difficulty navigating through the district's privacy regulations and lengthy data request process. ultimately, there was no easy solution to the problem: This evaluator did not get all of the data he wanted and had to make do with less. Still, he did receive a limited amount of coded student demographic and performance data and, by combining it with information from his other data collection activities, he was able to complete the study.

District protocols are just one layer of protection for sensitive student data; researchers also must abide by privacy laws and regulations at the state and federal levels. These protections can present obstacles for program evaluations, either by limiting evaluators' access to certain data sets or by requiring a rigorous or lengthy data request process. For some online program evaluators, the problem is exacerbated because they are studying student performance at multiple sites in different jurisdictions.

Title I Student Workshop Survey—Phoenix

At this time 12 responses have been received. 100% returned, 12 surveys deployed via e-mail.

Please select all that apply regarding the Phoenix student workshop. (Select all that apply)	Total Count	% of Total
My child enjoyed the student workshop.	10	83%
My child enjoyed socializing with peers at the workshop.	12	100%
The activities were varied.	10	83%
My child enjoyed working with the teachers.	11	92%
My child had a chance to learn some new math strategies.	8	67%
My child had the opportunity to review math skills.	10	83%
The activities were too hard.	0	0%
The activities were too easy.	1	8%

Please use the space below to let us know your thoughts about the student workshop. (Text limited to 250 characters.) (Text input)

Recipient	Response
	All 3 math teachers were very nice and understanding and they did not yell at you like the brick and mor-tar schools, which made learning fun.
	My son did not want to go when I took him. When I picked him up he told me he was glad he went.
	She was bored, "it was stuff she already knew," she stated. She liked the toothpick activity. She could have been challenged more. She LOVED lunch!
	My child really enjoyed the chance to work in a group setting. She seemed to learn a lot and the games helped things "click."
	She was happy she went and said she learned a lot and had lots of fun. That is what I was hoping for when I enrolled her. She is happy and better off for going.
	THANKS FOR THE WORKSHOP NEED MORE OF THEM
	The teachers were fun, smart and awesome, and the children learn new math strategies.
	Thank you keep up the good work.

Source: Arizona virtual Academy.

Figure 2. Example of Tabulated Results From an Arizona Virtual Academy Online Parent Survey About the Quality of a Recent Student Workshop.[19]

Of course, evaluators must adhere to all relevant privacy protections. To lessen impacts on the study's progress, researchers should consider privacy protections during the design phase and budget their time and money accordingly. Sometimes special arrangements also can be made to gain access to sensitive data while still protecting student privacy. Researchers might sign confidentiality agreements, physically travel to a specific site to analyze data (rather than have data released to them in electronic or hardcopy format), or even employ a neutral third party to receive data sets and strip out any identifying information before passing it to researchers.

Evaluators also can incorporate a variety of precautions in their own study protocol to protect students' privacy. In the Thinkport evaluation, for example, researchers scrupulously avoided all contact with students' names, referring to them only through a student identification number. The teachers participating in the study took attendance on a special form that included name and student identification number, then tore the names off the perforated page and mailed the attendance sheet to the evaluators. Through such procedures, evaluators can maintain students' privacy while still conducting the research needed to improve programs and instructional tools.

SUMMARY

As these examples show, program leaders and evaluators can often take proactive steps to avoid and address data collection problems. to ensure cooperation from study participants and boost data collection rates, they should build in plenty of time (and funds, if necessary) to communicate their evaluation goals with anyone in charge of collecting data from control groups. Program leaders also should communicate with students participating in evaluation studies, both to explain its goals, and to describe how students will benefit ultimately from the evaluation. these communication efforts should begin early and continue for the project's duration. additionally, program leaders should plan to offer incentives to data collectors and study participants.

Evaluators may want to consider administering surveys online, to boost response rates and easily compile results. In addition, there may be ways they can collect data electronically to better understand how online resources are used (e.g., by tracking different pathways users take as they navigate through a particular online tool or Web site, or how much time is spent on different portions of a Web site or online course).

When collecting data from multiple agencies, evaluators should consider in advance, the format and comparability of the data, making sure to define precisely what information should be collected and communicating these definitions to all those who are collecting and maintaining it.

Evaluators should research relevant privacy laws and guidelines well in advance and build in adequate time to navigate the process of requesting and collecting student data from states, districts, and schools. they may need to consider creative and flexible arrangements with agencies holding student data, and should incorporate privacy protections into their study protocol from the beginning, such as referring to students only through identification numbers.

Finally, if data collection problems cannot be avoided, and evaluators simply do not have what they need to complete a planned analysis, sometimes the best response is to redesign or refocus the evaluation. One strategy involves finding other sources of data that put more control into the hands of evaluators (e.g., observations, focus groups).

In: Evaluating Online Learning
Editor: Arthur T. Weston, pp. 63-67
ISBN 978-1-60741-107-9

Chapter 6

INTERPRETING THE IMPACT OF PROGRAM MATURITY

Online learning programs are often on the cutting edge of education reform and, like any new technology, may require a period of adaptation. For example, a district might try creating a new online course and discover some technical glitches when students begin to actually use it. Course creators also may need to fine-tune content, adjusting how it is presented or explained. For their part, students who are new to online course taking may need some time to get used to the format. Perhaps they need to learn new ways of studying or interacting with the teacher to be successful. If an evaluation is under way as all of this is going on, its findings may have more to do with the program's newness than its quality or effectiveness.

Because the creators of online programs often make adjustments to policies and practices while perfecting their model, it is ideal to wait until the program has had a chance to mature. at the same time, online learning programs are often under pressure to demonstrate effectiveness right away. although early evaluation efforts can provide valuable formative information for program improvement, they can sometimes be premature for generating reliable findings about effectiveness. Worse, if summative evaluations (see Glossary of Common Evaluation terms, p. 65) are undertaken too soon and show disappointing results, they could be damaging to programs' reputations or future chances at funding and political support.

What steps can evaluators and program leaders take to interpret appropriately the impact of the program's maturity on evaluation findings?

Several of the programs featured in this guide had evaluation efforts in place early on, sometimes from the very beginning. In a few cases, evaluators found less-than-positive outcomes at first and suspected that their findings were related to the program's lack of maturity. In these instances, the evaluators needed additional information to confirm their hunch and also needed to help program stakeholders understand and interpret the negative findings appropriately. In the case of thinkport, for example, evaluators designed a follow-up evaluation to provide more information about the program as it matured. In the case of the algebra I Online program, evaluators used multiple measures to provide stakeholders with a balanced perspective on the program's effectiveness.

CONDUCT FOLLOW-UP ANALYSES FOR DEEPER UNDERSTANDING

In evaluating the impact of thinkport's electronic field trip about slavery and the underground Railroad, evaluators from Macro International conducted a randomized controlled trial (see Glossary of Common Evaluation terms, p. 65), with the aim of understanding whether students who used this electronic field trip learned as much as students who received traditional instruction in the same content and did not use the field trip.

Initially, the randomized controlled trial revealed a disappointing finding: the electronic field trip did not impact student performance on a test of content knowledge any more or less than traditional instruction. a second phase of the study was initiated, however, when the evaluators dug deeper and analyzed whether teachers who had used an electronic field trip before were more successful than those using it for the first time. When they disaggregated the data, the evaluators found that students whose teachers were inexperienced with the electronic field trip actually learned less compared to students who received traditional instruction; however, students whose teachers had used the electronic field trip before learned more than the traditionally taught students. In the second semester, the evaluators were able to compare the effect of the treatment teachers using the electronic field trip for the first time to the effect of those same teachers using it a second time. this analysis found that when teachers used the electronic field trip a second time, its effectiveness rose dramatically. the students of teachers using the field trip a second time scored 121 percent higher on a test of knowledge about the underground Railroad than the students in the control group (see Glossary of Common Evaluation terms, p. 65) who had received traditional instruction on the same content.

The evaluators also looked at teachers' responses to open-ended survey questions to understand better why second-time users were so much more successful than first-timers. novice users reported that "they did not fully understand the Web site's capabilities when they began using it in their classes and that they were sometimes unable to answer student questions because they didn't understand the resource well enough themselves."[20] On the other hand, teachers that had used the electronic field trip once before "showed a deeper understanding of its resources and had a generally smoother experience working with the site."

In this instance, teachers needed time to learn how to integrate a new learning tool into their classrooms. although not successful at first, the teachers who got past the initial learning curve eventually became very effective in using the field trip to deliver content to students. this finding was important for two reasons. First, it suggested an area for program improvement: to counter the problem of teacher inexperience with the tool, the evaluators recommended that the program offer additional guidance for first-time users. Second, it kept the program's leaders from reaching a premature conclusion about the effectiveness of the Pathways to Freedom electronic field trip.

This is an important lesson, say thinkport's leaders, for them and others. as Helene Jennings, vice-president of Macro International, explains, "there's a lot of enthusiasm when something is developed, and patience is very hard for people. ... they want to get the results. It's a natural instinct." But, she says, it's important not to rush to summative judgments: "You just can't take it out of the box and have phenomenal success." Since the 2005 evaluation, the team has shared these experiences with other evaluators at several professional conferences. they do this, says Macro International Senior Manager Michael Long, to give other evaluators "ammunition" when they are asked to evaluate the effectiveness of a new technology too soon after implementation.

USE MULTIPLE MEASURES TO GAIN A BALANCED PERSPECTIVE

Teachers are not the only ones who need time to adapt to a new learning technology; students need time as well. Evaluators need to keep in mind that students' inexperience or discomfort with a new online course or tool also can cloud evaluation efforts—especially if an evaluation is undertaken early in the program's implementation. the algebra I Online program connects students to a certified algebra teacher via the Internet, while another teacher, who may or may not be certified, provides academic and technical support in the classroom. When comparing the experiences of algebra I Online students and traditional algebra students, EdC evaluators found mixed results. On the one hand, online students reported having less confidence in their algebra skills. Specifically, about two-thirds of students from the control group (those in traditional classes) reported feeling either confident or very confident in their algebra skills, compared to just under half of the algebra I Online students. the online students also were less likely to report having a good learning experience in their algebra class. about one-fifth of algebra I Online students reported that they did not have a good learning experience in the class, compared to only 6 percent of students in regular algebra classes. On the other hand, the online students showed achievement gains that were just as high or higher than those of traditional students. Specifically, the algebra I Online students outscored students in control classrooms on 18 of 25 posttest items, and they also tended to do better on those items that required them to create an algebraic expression from a real-world example.

In an article they published in the *Journal of Research on Technology in Education*, the evaluators speculated about why the online students were less confident in their algebra skills and had lower opinions of their learning experience: "It may be that the model of delayed feedback and dispersed authority in the online course led to a 'lost' feeling and prevented students from being able to gauge how they were doing."[21] In other words, without immediate reassurance from the teacher of record, students may have felt they weren't "getting it," when, in fact, they were.

This example suggests that students' unfamiliarity with a new program can substantially affect their perceptions and experiences. the evaluators in this case were wise to use a variety of measures to understand what students were experiencing in the class. taken alone, the students' reports about their confidence and learning experience could suggest that the algebra I Online program is not effective. But when the evaluators paired the self-reported satisfaction data with test score data, they were able to see the contradiction and gain a richer understanding of students' experiences in the program.

SUMMARY

A lack of program maturity is not a reason to forego evaluation. On the contrary, evaluation can be extremely useful in the early phases of program development. Even before a program is designed, evaluators can conduct needs assessments to determine how the target population can best be served. In the program's early implementation phase, evaluators can conduct formative evaluations that aim to identify areas for improvement. then, once users have had time to adapt, and program developers have had time to incorporate what they've learned from early feedback and observations, evaluators can turn to summative evaluations to determine effectiveness.

When disseminating findings from summative evaluations, program leaders should work with their evaluator to help program stakeholders understand and interpret how program maturity may have affected evaluation findings. the use of multiple measures can help provide a balanced perspective on the program's effectiveness. Program leaders also may want to consider repeating a summative evaluation to provide more information about the program as it matures.

Given the sophistication of many online learning programs today, it takes an extraordinary amount of time and money up front to create them. this, and stakeholders' eagerness for findings, makes these programs especially vulnerable to premature judgments. Evaluators have an important message to communicate to stakeholders: Evaluation efforts at all stages of development are critical to making sure investments are well spent, but they need to be appropriate for the program's level of maturity.

In: Evaluating Online Learning
Editor: Arthur T. Weston, pp. 69-77
ISBN 978-1-60741-107-9

Chapter 7

TRANSLATING EVALUATION FINDINGS INTO ACTION

As the phases of data collection and analysis wind down, work of another sort begins. Evaluators present their findings and, frequently, their recommendations; then program leaders begin the task of responding to them. Several factors contribute to the ease and success of this process: the strength of the findings, the clarity and specificity of the recommendations, how they are disseminated, and to whom. The relationship between the evaluators and the program leaders is key: When evaluators (external or internal) have ongoing opportunities to talk about and work with program staff on improvements, there is greater support for change. Conversely, if evaluators are fairly isolated from program leaders and leave the process once they have presented their recommendations, there is less support and, perhaps, a reduced sense of accountability among program staff. Of course, while frequent and open communication is important, maintaining objectivity and a respectful distance are also critical to obtaining valid research findings. Collaborations between researchers and practitioners should not be inappropriately close.

When program leaders try to act on evaluation findings, the structure and overall health of the organization play a role as well. Some program leaders meet with substantial barriers at this stage, particularly if they are trying to change the behavior of colleagues in scattered program sites or other offices or departments. The problem is compounded if there is a general lack of buy-in or familiarity with the evaluation.

In such circumstances, how can program leaders and evaluators translate findings into program improvements? Among the programs featured in this guide, there are a variety of approaches to using evaluation findings to effect change. In the CPS/vHS, for example, program leaders have used evaluation findings to persuade reluctant colleagues to make needed changes and have repeatedly returned to the evaluation recommendations to guide and justify internal decisions. Meanwhile, AZvA program staff use a structured, formal process for turning evaluation recommendations into program improvements, including establishing timelines, staff assignments, and regular status reports. The AZvA system, though time-consuming, has helped program administrators implement changes.

USE EVALUATION FINDINGS TO INFORM AND ENCOURAGE CHANGE

Chicago's CPS/vHS is managed and implemented collaboratively by three CPS offices: the Office of Technology Services eLearning, the Office of High School Programs, and the Office of Research, Evaluation, and Accountability. In 2005, Chief eLearning Officer Sharnell Jackson initiated an external evaluation to understand the cause of low course completion rates and find ways to help struggling students.

Evaluator Tom Clark of TA Consulting found great variation in students' ability to work independently, manage their time, and succeed without having an instructor physically present. The evaluation report recommended several ways to offer more support for struggling students, including having a dedicated class period in the school schedule for completing online course work and assigning on-site mentors to assist students during these periods. But when program administrators tried to implement these recommendations, they had difficulty compelling all participating schools to change. CPS is a large district with a distributed governance structure, making it difficult for the central office to force changes at the school-site level.

Facing resistance from schools, the program's administrators tried several different tacks to encourage implementation of the recommendations. First, they took every opportunity to communicate the evaluation findings to area administrators and principals of participating schools, making the case for change with credible data from an external source. Some school leaders resisted, saying they simply did not have the manpower or the funds to assign on-site mentors. Still, they could not ignore the compelling data showing that students needed help with pacing, study skills, and troubleshooting the technology; without this help many were failing. the strength of these findings, along with financial assistance from the district to provide modest stipends, convinced school site leaders to invest in mentors. Crystal Brown, senior analyst in CPS's Office of technology Services, reports that most CPS/vHS students now have access to an on-site mentor, "whereas before they just told a counselor, 'I want to enroll in this class,' and then they were on their own." Brown says the program leaders say the evaluation also has been useful for prodding principals to provide professional development for mentors and for persuading mentors to participate. they use the evaluation findings "whenever we train a mentor," she says, "and that's how we get a lot of buy-in."

CPS/vHS administrators also are careful to set a good example by using the evaluation findings and recommendations to guide their own practices at the central office. to date, they have implemented several "high priority" recommendations from the report. For example, program leaders strengthened mentor preparation by instituting quarterly trainings for mentors and establishing a shared online workspace that provides guidelines and advice for mentors. the district also has implemented advancement via Individual determination[22] programs in manyhigh schools to boost students' study skills and support their achievement in the online program. as CPS/vHS expands, some of the earlier problems have been avoided by getting site administrators to agree up front to the practices recommended by the evaluation. Brown says, "We constantly reiterate what this study recommended whenever we have any type of orientation [for] a new school that's enrolling."

Finally, in some instances, the program administrators changed program requirements outright and forced participating schools to comply. Beginning this year, for example, all online classes must have a regularly scheduled time during the school day. (there are a few exceptions made for very high-performing students.) this change ensures that students have dedicated computer time and mentor support to help them successfully complete their course work on time. In addition, participating students are now required to attend an orientation for the online courses where they receive training on study skills.

TAKE A STRUCTURED APPROACH TO IMPROVEMENT

Changing behavior and policy can be difficult in a large organization and, as the above example shows, program administrators must be creative and persistent to make it happen. Sometimes a small organization, such as an online school with a small central staff, has a distinct advantage when trying to implement evaluation recommendations. With a nimble staff and a strong improvement process in place, aZva, for example, has been especially effective in making program changes based on findings from its many evaluation efforts.

Several factors explain aZva's success in translating evaluation findings into program improvements. First, its evaluation process generates detailed recommendations from both outsiders and insiders. that is, staff from their main content provider, K12 Inc., visit aZva approximately every other year and conduct a quality assurance audit to identify areas for program improvement. Following the audit, K12 Inc. develops a series of recommendations and, in turn, aZva creates a detailed plan that shows what actions will be taken to address each recommendation, including who will be responsible and the target date for completion. For example, when the 2005 audit recommended that aZva create a formal feedback loop for teachers, the school assigned a staff member to administer monthly electronic surveys to collect information from teachers about the effectiveness of their professional development, their training and technology needs, their perceptions of parent training needs, and their suggestions for enhancing community relations. aZva has responded in similar fashion to many other recommendations generated by K12 Inc.'s site visit, addressing a range of organizational, instructional, and operational issues (see table 4, Excerpts From aZva's next Steps Plan, in Response to Recommendations From the K12 Quality assurance audit, p. 47).

In addition to the audit, K12 Inc. also requires that aZva complete an annual School Improvement Plan (SIP), which consists of two parts: a self-evaluation of school operations in general and a Student achievement Improvement Plan (SaIP) that specifically focuses on student outcomes. In developing these plans, aZva staff articulate a series of goals and specific objectives for improvement, again including strategies and timelines for meeting each objective. a strength of this process is its specificity. For example, one key SaIP goal was to improve student achievement in math, and the administrative team set the specific goal of decreasing by 5 percent the number of students who score "far below the standards" on the state standards test and increasing by 5 percent the number who meet or exceed state standards. to accomplish this, aZva staff took action on several fronts: they aligned their curriculum to the state's testing blueprint, developed a new curriculum sequencing plan, implemented additional teacher and parent training, worked with students to encourage test preparation and participation, and developed individual math learning plans for students.

Table 4. Excerpts From AZVA's Next Steps Plan, In Response to Recommendations From the K1 2 Quality Assurance Audit[23]

K1 2 Inc. Site Visit Recommenda- tions	Actions	Time- line	Respon- sible	Status
Board and Organizational Structure				
AZVA should create additional mecha- nisms to centralize communications	The AZVA administration will survey school staff to de- termine communications needs. The administration will evaluate technology to assist with centralizing communications. The administration will develop a communications plan and begin implementation in fall 2005.	12/31/20 05	Janice Grune- berg	Will begin in summer 2005
AZVA should create a formal feedback loop with teachers	The AZVA administration will develop a survey instrument to collect information from teachers regarding the effective- ness of professional development, outside training needs and effectiveness of outside training opportunities, technology needs, parent training needs, and community relations suggestions. The survey will be administered at monthly professional development meetings and available in an electronic format to capture contemporaneous feedback.	8/1/2005	Jacque Johnson -Hirt	Will begin develop ment in July

Table 4. Continued

K1 2 Inc. Site Visit Recommendations	Actions	Time-line	Respon-sible	Status
Instruction				
AZVA should consider designing new teacher training and ongoing teacher training for each year in chunks and stages, rather than as one long week of training; this structure would allow practice and reflection.	The director of instruction is developing the new teacher training agenda and sessions. Summer projects will be assigned in May; lead teachers will work with the director of instruction to develop training modules.	8/1/2005	Jacque Johnson -Hirt	On track to meet timeline
As AZVA continues to grow, it should give attention to scalability in all initia- tives from teacher mentoring and group Professional Development and training to student work samples.	The director of instruction is revising the Parent Orientation Guide (includes work sample guidelines). Lead teachers and regular education teachers will have summer projects based on teacher training and mentoring needs.	8/1/2005	Jacque Johnson -Hirt	On track to meet timeline
AZVA should consider a way for admin- istration to review aggregate views of low-performing students as the school continues to grow (one suggestion could be having teachers submit the aggregate view,	AZVA administration has requested a part-time adminis- trative position to manage and analyze student-level data. The administration has also requested a formal registrar position to capture data on incoming students. The assis- tant director for operations is revising the teacher	9/15/2005	Janice Gruneberg, Jacque Johnson -Hirt	On track to meet timeline

highlighted with red or yellow depending on level of attention needed).	tracking tool with this goal in mind.			
Community Relations				
AZVA should continue to develop ways to encourage students and parents to attend outings and encourage increased participation in school activities.	The director of instruction is working with teachers to de- velop lesson-based outings based on parent feedback. A master outing schedule and plans will be developed and included in the revised Parent Orientation Guide.	7/30/200 5	Jacque Johnson -Hirt	Adminis trative team is making summer project assign- ments in May; on track to meet timeline
Special Education				
AZVA should monitor the special educa- tion students' state test scores from year to year in correlation with their IEP goals to ensure proper growth as well as comparable growth to same age non-disabled peers.	The administration is requesting a part-time staff position to manage and analyze student-level data. The SPED team is currently developing a process to measure prog- ress on IEP goals, including test score gains. State test scores will be available in June.	7/15/200 5	Lisa Walker	SPED team developi ng process; on track to meet timeline

Another strength of aZva's process is that it requires program staff to review evaluation recommendations regularly and continually track the progress that has been made toward them. the SIP and SaIP are evolving plans that are regularly updated and revised by "basically everyone that has any role in instruction," such as the director of instruction, the high school director, and the special education manager, says aZva's director, Mary Gifford. as part of this process, team members continually return to the document and track how much progress has been made in reaching their goals. there also is external accountability for making progress on SIP and SaIP goals: approximately once a quarter, aZva staff review the plans via conference calls with K12 Inc.

Finally, aZva's approach succeeds because it permeates the work of the entire school. as Bridget Schleifer, the K–8 principal, explains, "Evaluation is built into everybody's role and responsibility." Staff members at all levels are expected to take evaluation recommendations seriously and to help to implement changes based on them.

Summary

As the above examples show, whether and how evaluation findings lead to program improvements is a function not only of the quality of the evaluation, but of many other contextual and organizational factors. Program leaders can facilitate program change by working from the beginning to create an ongoing relationship between evaluators and program staff. throughout the process, there should be opportunities for staff members to discuss the evaluation, its findings, and its implications for improving the program. Off-site staff and partners should be included as well. In short, program leaders should communicate early and often about the evaluation with anyone whose behavior might be expected to change as a result of its findings.

Once findings and recommendations are available, program leaders might want to consider using a structured, formal process for turning those recommendations into program improvements. One approach is to decide on a course of action, set a timeline, and identify who will be responsible for implementation. Whether using a formal process or not, program leaders should revisit recommendations regularly and continually track the progress that has been made toward them.

In some instances, recommended changes to an online program or resource may be technically hard to implement. For example, it may be difficult and expensive to make changes to the content or format of an online course. It also may be quite costly to change, repair, or provide the hardware needed to improve an online program. Insufficient funding may cause other difficulties as well. If the program has relied on external funding that has subsequently run out, there may be pressure to dilute the program's approach; for example, districts might feel pressured to keep an online course but eliminate the face-to-face mentors that support students as they proceed through it.

Online program evaluators need to keep these kinds of practical challenges in mind when formulating recommendations and should consider ranking their suggestions both in order of importance and feasibility. Program leaders should develop a plan for addressing the highest priority recommendations first. In situations where program funds are running low, evaluators can provide a much-needed external perspective, reminding stakeholders of the project's goals and helping them identify the most critical program elements to keep, even if it means serving fewer participants. More broadly, communication and persistence are essential when attempting to translate evaluation findings into action.

PART II: RECOMMENDATIONS FOR EVALUATING ONLINE LEARNING

Part I draws on seven featured evaluations to illustrate the challenges of evaluating online learning and to describe how different evaluators have addressed them. Part II offers recommendations that synthesize the lessons learned in these examples and also draw from research and conversations with experts in evaluating online learning. these recommendations aim to provide guidance to program leaders who are contemplating an evaluation and to assist program leaders and evaluators who are already working together to complete one.

In: Evaluating Online Learning
Editor: Arthur T. Weston, pp. 81-89
ISBN 978-1-60741-107-9

Chapter 8

GENERAL RECOMMENDATIONS

Several recurring themes can be found in the seven featured evaluations, as well as in the research and comments from experts in the field of online learning. these sources point to a handful of overarching recommendations:

- Begin with a clear vision for the evaluation. determine what you want the evaluation to accomplish and what questions you hope to answer. Program leaders and evaluators may want to consider the questions listed in the box on page 51 as they get started.
- Determine the most appropriate evaluation methods for meeting your goals. Consider the different types of evaluations discussed in the guide (see Part I for examples of formative and summative; internal and external; experimental, quasi-experimental, and other types of evaluations) and the costs and benefits of each. What type of evaluation is appropriate given your stated purpose? What research methods will best capture program effects?
- Budget to meet evaluation needs. Limited budgets are a common barrier to evaluators. When designing evaluations, consider whether there are available funds to cover all planned data collection and analysis activities, plus the costs of any needed background research, internal communications and reporting, and incentives for study participants. If available funds are not sufficient, scale back the evaluation and focus on the highest-priority activities.
- Develop a program culture that supports evaluation. discuss evaluation with staff members, clearly explaining its value and their roles in collecting and analyzing data. Incorporate data collection and analysis

activities into staff members' everyday responsibilities instead of treating these tasks as one-time efforts or burdens. Make external evaluators less threatening to program staff members by creating opportunities for dialogue between the evaluator and program leaders and staff. Incorporate evaluation data into the process of development of annual program goals and strategic planning activities.

- Communicate early and often with anyone who will be affected by the evaluation.
- Dedicate adequate time and money to communicating with internal and external stakeholders at all phases of the evaluation. However, be sensitive to program concerns about keeping evaluation results confidential and avoiding media scrutiny. Always keep those managing the program "in the loop." Communicating through the program director is often the best course of action.

Recommendations for Meeting the Needs of Multiple Stakeholders

- Identify up front the various stakeholders who will be interested in the evaluation and what specifically they will want to know. Consider conducting interviews or focus groups to collect this information.
- Use this information to determine the evaluation's main purpose(s) and to develop questions that will guide the study. An evaluation that clearly addresses stakeholder needs and interests is more likely to yield findings and recommendations they will find worthy and champion.
- If trying to fulfill both program improvement and accountability purposes, consider using evaluation approaches that can generate both formative and summative information (see Glossary of Common Evaluation terms, p. 65). Be realistic at this stage and keep in mind the constraints of the evaluation budget and timeline.
- Think early on about how the evaluation will incorporate student learning outcomes for accountability purposes. Consider a range of academic outcomes that might be appropriate to study, including scores on state-mandated and other standardized tests, course completions, grades, and on-time graduation.

- If the program has multiple components, determine the ones with the best potential to have a direct measurable impact on student achievement, and focus your study of student outcomes there.
- Consider using "dashboard indicators," the two or three most critical goals to be measured. How can the measures be succinctly communicated? Can they be graphed over time to demonstrate improved performance over time? (For example, an online program trying to increase access to Advanced Placement (AP)[24] courses might have a dashboard indicator composed of the number of schools accessing online AP courses, the AP exam pass rate, and the number of students taking AP exams as a percentage of total number of AP students in online AP courses.)
- In the reporting phase, think about what findings will be of most interest to different stakeholders. Consider communicating findings to different audiences in ways that are tailored to their needs and interests.
- If already participating in mandatory evaluation activities, think about how those findings can be used for other purposes, such as making internal improvements. disseminate any mandatory evaluation reports to the staff and discuss how their findings can be used to strengthen the program. Consider developing additional data collection efforts to supplement the mandatory evaluation.

Recommendations for Utilizing and Building on the Existing Base of Knowledge

- Look to established standards for online learning to determine elements of high- quality programs.
- Program evaluation has a long history, and its basic approaches can be adapted to fit any unique educational program. the *Program Evaluation Standards* (1994) from the Joint Committee on Standards for Educational Evaluation and other guides (see Evaluation Methods and tools in appendix A) can be helpful to those developing an online learning evaluation.
- Don't reinvent the wheel unless you have to—consult the list of distance education and evaluation resources in appendix A and identify program peers you can contact about their evaluation activities.

- Participate in the community of evaluators and researchers studying K–1 2 online learning. Share evaluation tools and processes with others. Make them available online. Consider publishing in professional journals. Seek out networking venues such as conferences.

Important Questions for K–12 Online Learning Evaluators and Practitioners

In a synthesis of research on K–12 online learning, Rosina Smith of the Alberta Online Consortium, Tom Clark of TA Consulting, and Robert Blomeyer of Blomeyer & Clemente Consulting Services developed a list of important questions for researchers of K–12 online learning to consider.[25] That list, which drew from the work of Cathy Cavanaugh et al.,[26] has been adapted here for program and evaluation practitioners. Of course, no evaluation can cover all of these questions; this list is meant to provide a starting point for discussing evaluation goals and topics of interest.

Learner outcomes. What is the impact of the K–1 2 online learning program on student achievement? What factors can increase online course success rates? What impact does the program have on learner process skills, such as critical and higher-order thinking? How are learner satisfaction and motivation related to outcomes?

Learner characteristics. What are the characteristics of successful learners in this K–1 2 online learning program, and can success be predicted? How do learner background, preparation, and screening influence academic outcomes in the program?

Online learning features. What are the most effective combinations of media and methods in the online learning program? How do interaction, collaboration, and learner pacing influence academic outcomes? What is the impact of the K–1 2 online learning program when used as a supplement, in courses, or in full programs of study?

Online teaching and professional development. What are the characteristics of successful teachers in this K–1 2 online learning program? Are the training, mentoring, and support systems for these teachers effective?

Education context. What kinds of programs and curricula does the K–1 2 online learning program offer? How can the program best be used to improve learner outcomes in different content areas, grade levels, and academic programs? How can it help participating schools meet NCLB requirements? How do resources, policy, and funding impact the success of the program? Can an effective model of K–1 2 online learning be scaled up and sustained by the program?

- Use caution when interpreting evaluation findings from other programs, or adapting their methods. Online learning programs "come in many shapes and sizes," and findings about one online program or set of Web resources are not always generalizable. take time to understand the program being studied and its context before deciding if the findings or methods are relevant and appropriate.
- If developing new tools for collecting data or new processes for analyzing it, work collaboratively with leaders of similar programs or experts from other agencies to fill gaps in knowledge.

RECOMMENDATIONS FOR EVALUATING MULTIFACETED RESOURCES

- Multifaceted programs include a range of program activities and may struggle to define a clear, central purpose. Evaluators can help such programs define and refine their purposes and goals. Establishing key performance measures aligned to funder-mandated and project goals can help program managers prioritize and help evaluators identify what is most important to study.
- When evaluating a multifaceted educational program, consider an evaluation strategy that combines both breadth and depth. For example, collect broad information about usage and select a particular program feature or resource to examine more deeply.
- Where feasible, consider a multiyear evaluation plan that narrows its focus in each successive year, or examines a different resource each year.
- to select a particular program feature or resource for deeper examination, think about what each resource is intended to do, or what outcomes one would hope to see if the resource was being used effectively. Work with an evaluator to determine which resource is best suited for a more thorough evaluation.

RECOMMENDATIONS FOR PROGRAMS CONSIDERING A COMPARISON STUDY

- Seek to determine if a comparison study is appropriate, and, if it is, whether there is a viable way to compare program participants with others. Consider the online program's goals, the student population being served, and the program's structure. For example, online programs dedicated to credit recovery would not want to compare their student outcomes with those of the general student population.
- Clearly articulate the purpose of the comparison. Is the evaluation seeking to find out if the online program is *just as* effective as the traditional one or *more* effective? For example, "just as effective" findings are desirable and appropriate when online programs are being used to expand education access.
- If considering a quasi-experimental design (see Glossary of Common Evaluation terms, p. 65), plan carefully for what classes will be used as control groups, and thoroughly assess the ways they are similar to and different from the treatment classes. What kinds of students does each class serve? did the students (or teachers) choose to participate in the class or were they assigned to it randomly? are students taking the treatment and control classes for similar reasons (e.g., credit recovery, advanced learning)? are the students at a similar achievement level? Where feasible, use individual student record data to match treatment and comparison students or to hold constant differences in prior learning characteristics across the two groups.
- If considering a randomized controlled trial (see Glossary of Common Evaluation terms, p. 65), determine how feasible it is for the particular program. Is it possible to assign students randomly either to receive the treatment or be in the control group? Other practical considerations: Can the control group students receive the treatment at a future date? What other incentives can be offered to encourage them to participate? Will control and treatment students be in the same classroom or school? If so, might this cause "contamination" between treatment and control groups?
- In the event a randomized controlled trial or quasi-experimental study is planned, plan to offer meaningful incentives to participating individuals and schools. When deciding on appropriate incentives, consider the total time commitment that will be asked of study participants.

- Study sites with no vested financial interest are more likely to withdraw or to fail to carry through with study requirements that differ from typical school practices. If compliance appears unlikely, do not attempt an experimental or quasi-experimental study, unless it is an explicit requirement of a mandated evaluation.
- When designing data management systems, keep in mind the possibility of comparisons with traditional settings. Collect and organize data in a way that makes such comparisons possible.

Recommendations for Gathering Valid Evaluation Data

- Build in adequate time to fully communicate the purpose and design of the evaluation to everyone involved. Inform program staff who will play a role in the evaluation, as well as anyone who will help you gather evaluation evidence. Explain how study participants will benefit from the evaluation.
- Be prepared to repurpose the methods you use to conduct an evaluation, without losing sight of the evaluation's original purpose. Collecting multiple sources of evidence related to the same evaluation question can help to ensure that the evaluator can answer the question if a data source becomes unavailable or a research method proves infeasible.
- Seek out valid and reliable instruments for gathering data. Existing data-gathering instruments that have been tested and refined can offer higher-quality data than locally developed instruments.
- Consider administering surveys online, to boost response rates and easily compile results.
- Consider if there are innovative ways to collect data electronically about how online resources are used (e.g., tracking different pathways users take as they navigate through a particular online tool or Web site, or how much time is spent on different portions of a Web site or online course).
- If response rates are too low, consider redesigning or refocusing the evaluation. Find other indicators that get at the same phenomenon. Find other data sources that put more control into the hands of evaluators (e.g., observations, focus groups).
- If collecting and aggregating data across multiple sources, define indicators clearly and make sure that data are collected in compatible

formats. define exactly what is to be measured, and how, and distribute these instructions to all parties who are collecting data.

- Research relevant data privacy regulations well in advance.
- Determine the process and build in adequate time for requesting student data from states, districts, or schools. determine early on whether data permissions will be needed and from whom, and how likely it is that sensitive data will actually be available. Have a "Plan B" if it is not.
- If the program does not have good access to the complete school record of enrolled students, encourage it to support school improvement and program evaluator needs by collecting *NCLB* subgroup and other key student record data as part of its regular program registration process.
- Consider creative and flexible arrangements for protecting student privacy (e.g., sign confidentiality agreements, physically travel to a specific site to analyze data, employ a disinterested third party to receive data sets and strip out any identifying information).
- Incorporate precautions into the study protocol to protect students' privacy. When possible, avoid contact with students' names and refer to students through student identification numbers.

RECOMMENDATIONS FOR TAKING PROGRAM MATURITY INTO ACCOUNT

- All education programs go through developmental stages. different kinds of evaluation are appropriate at each stage.[27] Based on when they started and other factors, different components of a program may be in different development stages during an evaluation.
- In the early stages of implementation, focus on formative evaluation efforts. Hold off on summative evaluations until users have had time to adapt to it, and there has been adequate time to revise the program design based on early feedback and observations.
- Once a stable program model has been achieved, study of education outcomes is appropriate. Finally, as the program or program component matures, its long-term sustainability and replicability should be considered.
- Program leaders and evaluators should work together to help program stakeholders understand and interpret how program maturity can affect evaluation findings.

- Program leaders and evaluators should work together to establish baselines and benchmarks, so that progress over time toward program goals can be measured.

Recommendations for Translating Evaluation Findings into Action

Online learning programs often exist within larger learning organizations and policy and practice frameworks that encourage or inhibit program success. use evaluation results to encourage needed changes in program context.

- Key stakeholders, such as parents and students, teachers, schools, administrators, policymakers, and the general public, can be informed through the communication of evaluation results. Communication of evaluation results can help online learning programs demonstrate their value or worth, demonstrate accountability, and dispel myths about the nature of online learning.
- If the resulting recommendations are actionable, online learning programs should move quickly to implement them. don't just file the evaluation away; make it a living document that informs the program.
- Work to create an ongoing relationship among evaluators, program leaders, and staff. Create ongoing opportunities to talk about the evaluation, its findings, and its implications for improving the program.
- Engage early with anyone whose behavior will be expected to change as a result of the evaluation findings—including personnel at distant sites who help manage the program. Introduce them to evaluators and communicate the purpose of the evaluation.
- Institutionalize process improvement and performance measurement practices put in place during the evaluation. Consider using a structured, formal process for turning evaluation recommendations into program improvements, including timelines and staff assignments.
- Review evaluation recommendations regularly and continually track the progress that has been made toward them.
- Rank evaluation recommendations both in order of importance and feasibility. develop a plan for addressing the highest priority recommendations first.

- Continue to conduct evaluation activities internally or externally to continuously improve your program over time.

In: Evaluating Online Learning
Editor: Arthur T. Weston, pp. 91-95

ISBN 978-1-60741-107-9

Chapter 9

FEATURED ONLINE LEARNING EVALUATIONS

ALABAMA CONNECTING CLASSROOMS, EDUCATORS, AND STUDENTS STATEWIDE DISTANCE LEARNING

Alabama

The Alabama Connecting Classrooms, Educators, & Students Statewide (ACCESS) distance Learning Initiative aims to provide all Alabama high school students "equal access to high quality instruction to improve student achievement." ACCESS was developed to support and expand existing distance learning initiatives in Alabama and to heighten their impact on student achievement. In particular, the aim was to provide more courses to students in small and rural schools. ACCESS courses are Web-based, utilize interactive videoconferencing (IvC) platforms, or combine both technologies. ACCESS offers courses in core subjects, plus foreign languages, electives, remedial courses, and advanced courses, including Advanced Placement (AP)[28] and dual credit courses. the courses are developed and delivered by Alabama-certified teachers. In addtion to distance learning courses for students, ACCESS also provides teachers with professional development and multimedia tools to enhance instruction. ACCESS is coordinated by the Alabama State department of Education and three regional support centers. By the end of 2006, ACCESS was serving almost 4,000 online users and over 1,000 IvC users and, ultimately, is intended to reach all public high schools in the state.

ALGEBRA I ONLINE

Louisiana

Algebra I Online began as a program under the Louisiana virtual School, an initiative of the Louisiana department of Education that provides the state's high school students with access to standards-based high school courses delivered by certified Louisiana teachers via the Internet. the program has two goals: to increase the number of students taught by highly qualified algebra teachers, especially in rural and urban areas, and to help uncertified algebra teachers improve their skills and become certified. In Algebra I Online courses, students participate n a face-to-face class that meets at their home school as part of the regular school day, and each student has a computer connected to the Internet. A teacher who may or may not be certified to deliver algebra instruction is physically present in the classroom to facilitate student learning, while a highly qualified, certified teacher delivers the algebra instruction online. the online instructor's responsibilities include grading assignments and tests, and submitting course grades; the in-class teacher oversees the classroom and works to create an effective learning environment. the online and in-class teachers communicate regularly during the year to discuss student progress. the algebra course is standards-aligned and incorporates e-mail, interactive online components, and video into the lessons. By the 2005–06 school year, 350 students in 20 schools were taking Algebra I Online courses, and five participating teachers had earned secondary mathematics certification.

APPLETON ESCHOOL

Wisconsin

Based in Wisconsin's Appleton Area School district, Appleton eSchool is an online charter high school intended to provide high-quality, self-paced online courses. A few students choose to take their entire high school course load through Appleton eSchool, but most use the online courses to supplement those available at their home school. the school is open to all district high school students, but it makes special efforts to include those with significant life challenges. Appleton eSchool offers core subjects, electives (e.g., art, economics, Web design, "thinking and learning strategies"), and AP courses. Students can gain access to their Web-based courses around the clock and submit their assignments via the Internet. they can communicate with teachers using e-mail and online discussions, and receive oral assessments and tutoring by telephone and Web conference tools. teachers regularly communicate student progress with a contact at the student's local school and with each student's mentor (usually the student's parent), whose role is to provide the student with assistance and encouragement. By 2007–08, the school was serving 275 students enrolled in over 500 semester courses. In addition, the 2007 summer session included another 400 semester course enrollments.

ARIZONA VIRTUAL ACADEMY

Arizona

Arizona virtual Academy (AZvA) is a public charter school serving students in grades kindergarten through 11 across Arizona. By 2006–07, AZvA was serving approximately 2,800 students up through the 10th grade and piloting a small 11th-grade program. AZvA offers a complete selection of core, elective, and AP courses, including language arts, math, science, history, art, music, and physical education. Courses are developed by veteran public and private school teachers and supplied to AZvA by a national curriculum provider, K12 Inc. In 2006–07, AZvA used title I funds[29] to add a supplemental math program for struggling students in grades 3 through 8. In all AZvA courses, certified teachers provide instruction and keep track of students' progress. Students participate in structured activities, and also study independently under the guidance of an assigned mentor. When families enroll with AZvA, the program sends them curricular materials, accompanying textbooks and workbooks, supplemental equipment and supplies, and a computer and printer, the latter two on loan. Students are assessed regularly, both for placement in the appropriate course level and to determine their mastery of course content.

Chicago Public Schools' Virtual High School

Chicago

The Chicago Public Schools' virtual High School (CPS/vHS) is intended to expand access to high- quality teachers and courses, especially for students who traditionally have been underserved. The program is a partnership with the Illinois virtual High School (IvHS)—a well-established distance learning program serving the entire state. CPS/vHS offers a variety of online courses. To participate, students must meet prerequisites and are advised of the commitment they will need to make to succeed in the class. CPS/vHS leaders are clear that, in this program, *online* does not mean independent study: Courses run for a semester, students are typically scheduled to work online during the regular school day, and attendance during that time is required. On- site mentors are available to help students as they progress through the online classes. Despite this regular schedule, the program still offers flexibility and convenience not available in a traditional system because students can communicate with instructors and access course materials outside of regular class hours. Today, CPS/vHS offers over 100 online courses, and new classes are added when the district determines that the course will meet the needs of approximately 60 to 75 students.

Digital Learning Commons

Washington

Based in the state of Washington, the Digital Learning Commons (DLC) is a centrally hosted Web portal that offers a wide range of services and resources to students and teachers. DLC's core goal is to offer education opportunities and choices where they have not previously existed due to geographic or socioeconomic barriers. Through DLC, middle and high school students can access over 300 online courses, including all core subjects and various electives, plus Advanced Placement and English as a Second Language classes. DLC students also have access to online student mentors (made possible through university partnerships), and college and career-planning resources. DLC hosts an extensive digital library, categorized by subject area, for students, teachers, and parents. In addition, it includes resources and tools for teachers, including online curricula, activities, and diagnostics. It is integrated with Washington's existing

K–20 Network—a high-speed telecommunications infrastructure that allows Washington's K–12 schools to use the Internet and interactive videoconferencing. When schools join DLC, program staff help them create a plan for using the portal to meet their needs and, also, provide training to help school faculty and librarians incorporate its resources into the classroom.

THINKPORT

Maryland

Maryland Public Television has partnered with Johns Hopkins university Center for Technology in Education to create Thinkport, a Web site that functions as a one-stop shop for teacher nd student resources. thinkport brings together quality educational resources and tools from trusted sources, including the Library of Congress, the u.S. department of Education, PBS, the Kennedy Center, the national Council of teachers of English, national Geographic, and the Smithsonian Institution. the site is organized into four sections: classroom resources, career resources for teachers, instructional technology, and family and community resources. about 75 percent of the site's content is for teachers, including lesson plans and activities for students, all of which include a technology component. thinkport also offers podcasts, video clips, blogs, and games, with accompanying information about how they can be used effectively in classrooms. One of thinkport's most popular features is its collection of electronic field trips—a number of which were developed by Maryland Public television under the u.S. department of Education's Star Schools grant, a federal program that supports distance learning projects for teachers and students in underserved populations. Each field trip is essentially an online curricular unit that focuses in depth on a particular topic and includes many interactive components for students and accompanying support materials for teachers.

In: Evaluating Online Learning
Editor: Arthur T. Weston, pp. 97-102
ISBN 978-1-60741-107-9

Appendix A: Resources

The resources listed below are intended to provider readers with ready access to further information about evaluating online learning. This is not a complete list, and there may be other useful resources on the topic. Selection was based on the criteria that resources be relevant to the topic and themes of this guide; current and up-to-date; from nationally recognized organizations, including but not limited to federal or federally funded sources; and that they offer materials free of charge. This listing offers a range of research, practical tools, policy information, and other resources.

Distance Learningh

International Society of Technology in Education

The International Society of Technology in Education (ISTE) is a nonprofit organization with more than 85,000 members. ISTE provides services, including evaluation, to improve teaching, learning, and school leadership through the use of technology. In 2007, ISTE published a comprehensive overview of effective online teaching and learning practices, *What Works in K–12 Online Learning*. Chapter topics include virtual course development, online learning in elementary classrooms, differentiating instruction online, professional development for teachers of virtual courses, and the challenges that virtual schools will face in the future.

http://www.iste.org

The North American Council for Online Learning

The north American Council for Online Learning (nACOL) is an international K–12 nonprofit organization focused on enhancing K–12 online learning quality. nACOL publications, programs, and research areas include the *National Standards of Quality for Online Courses, National Standards for Quality Online Teaching*, state needs assessments for online courses and services, online course quality evaluations, online professional development, virtual education program administration, funding, and state and federal public policy. In addition, nACOL has published a primer on K–12 online learning, which includes information about teaching, learning, and curriculum in online environments, and evaluating online learning.

http://www.nacol.org

North Central Regional Educational Laboratory/ Learning Point Associates

The north Central Regional Educational Laboratory (nCREL) was a federally funded education laboratory until 2005. Learning Point Associates conducted the work of nCREL and now operates a regional educational laboratory (REL) with a new scope of work and a new name: REL Midwest. nCREL publications about online learning are currently available on the Learning Point Associates Web site, including *A Synthesis of New Research on K–12 Online Learning* (2005), which summarizes a series of research projects sponsored by nCREL and includes recommendations for online research, policy, and practice.

http://www.ncrel.org/tech/elearn.htm

Southern Regional Education Board

The Southern Regional Education Board (SREB) is a nonprofit organization that provides education reform resources to its 16 member states. The SREB Educational Technology Cooperative focuses on ways to help state leaders create and expand the use of technology in education. SREB's Web site provides the *Standards for Quality Online Courses* and *Standards for Quality Online Teaching*. In 2005, SREB partnered with the AT&T Foundation to create the State virtual Schools Alliance, to assist SREB's 16 member states to increase middle- and high- school students' access to rigorous academic courses through state-supported virtual schools. Through AT&T Foundation grant funding, the alliance facilitates collaboration and information and resource sharing between states in order to create and improve state virtual schools.

http://www.sreb.org

Star Schools Program

The Star Schools Program, housed in the u.S. department of Education's Office of Innovation and Improvement, supports distance education programs that encourage improved instruction across subjects and bring technology to underserved populations. Information about the program and its evaluation is available on the department of Education's Web site. The Star Schools Program is funding this guide.

http://www.ed.gov/programs/starschools/ index.html

Evaluation Methods and Tools

Institute of Education Sciences

In 2002, the *Education Sciences Reform Act* created the Institute of Education Sciences (IES) as an institute dedicated to conducting and providing research, evaluation, and statistics in the education field. IES maintains a registry of evaluators and has published the two guides described below. The Regional Educational Laboratory Program is also housed within IES.

http://ies.ed.gov

Identifying and Implementing Educational Practices Supported by Rigorous Evidence: A User Friendly Guide

Published by the u.S. department of Education, this guide is meant to help practitioners understand the meaning of "rigorous evidence" and important research and evaluation terms, such as "randomized controlled trials." under-standing these terms and the different types of evidence in the education field can help when designing an internal evaluation or working with an external agency.

http://www.ed.gov/rschstat/research/pubs/ rigorousevid/index.html

Random Assignment in Program Evaluation and Intervention Research: Questions and Answers

This document, published by the Institute of Education Sciences in the u.S. department of Education, discusses the purpose of education program evaluation generally, and answers specific questions about studies that use random assignment to determine program effectiveness.

http://ies.ed.gov/ncee/pubs/randomqa.asp

Regional Educational Laboratory Program

The Regional Educational Laboratory (REL) Program is a network of 10 applied research laboratories that serve the education needs of the states within a designated region by providing access to scientifically valid research, studies, and other related technical assistance services. The labs employ researchers experienced in scientific evaluations who can provide technical assistance on evaluation design. The REL Web site provides contact information for each of the labs.

http://ies.ed.gov/ncee/edlabs/regions

Local School System Planning, Implementation, and Evaluation Guide

This guide from Maryland virtual Learning Opportunities is a useful resource when considering program implementation. Planning considerations are divided into a three-part checklist of planning, implementation, and evaluation. Additionally, suggested roles and responsibilities are provided for both district- and school- based personnel. The guide can be found online at the following uRL, using the link on the left-hand side for the "Planning, Implementation, and Evaluation Guide."

http://mdk12online.org/docs/PIEGuide.pdf

Online Program Perceiver Instrument

The Online Program Perceiver Instrument OPPI) was designed by the staff at Appleton eSchool in Wisconsin, as an online evaluation tool to be used by

Wisconsin's network of virtual schools. the tool is featured as an internal evaluation process in this guide and is currently available for all online learning programs across the country to use. the Web site provides information about the framework and an overview of how the instrument works, as well as contact information and directions on how to become a member of the OPPI network.

http://www.wisconsineschool.net/OPPI/OPPI. asp

Program Evaluation Standards

This document is a 1994 publication of the Joint Committee on Standards for Educational Evaluation, a coalition of professional associations concerned with the quality of evaluation. the standards address utility, feasibility, proprietary, and accuracy issues, and are intended for use in checking the design and operation of an evaluation.

http://www.wmich.edu/evalctr/jc

2005 SETDA National Leadership Institute Tool- kit on Virtual Learning

The State Educational technology directors Association (SEtdA) was developed to provide national leadership and facilitate collaboration between states on education technology issues. Each year, SEtdA hosts a national Leadership Institute and develops toolkits intended to help educators effectively use virtual learning. the 2004–05 toolkit includes a lengthy section on program evaluation.

http://www.setda.org/toolkit/toolkit2004/ index.htm

Resources from Higher Education

Council for Higher Education Accreditation

The Council for Higher Education Accreditation (CHEA) has a number of publications identifying standards and best practices in distance learning. these include: *Accreditation and Assuring Quality in Distance Learning* and *Best*

Practices for Electronically Offered Degree and Certificate Programs, available at the following Web sites, respectively:

http://www.chea.org/Research/ Accred-Distance-5-9-02.pdf http://www.ncahlc.org/download/Best_Pract_ DEd.pdf

Quality Matters

Quality Matters is a multi-partner project funded in part by the u.S. department of Education's Fund for the Improvement of Postsecondary Education (FIPSE). Quality Matters has created a rubric and process for certifying the quality of online courses.

http://www.qualitymatters.org/index.htm

Sloan Consortium

The Sloan Consortium (Sloan-C) is a consortium of institutions and organizations committed to quality online education. It aims to help learning organizations improve the quality of their programming, and has a report identifying five "pillars" of quality higher education online programs: learning effectiveness, student satisfaction, faculty satisfaction, cost effectiveness, and access. Sloan-C also has a Web site that collects information about best practices within each of these areas.

http://www.sloan-c.org

These pages identify resources created and maintained by other public and private organizations. This information is provided for the reader's convenience. The U.S. Department of Education is not responsible for controlling or guaranteeing the accuracy, relevance, timeliness, or completeness of this outside information. Further, the inclusion of these resources does not reflect their importance, nor is it intended to endorse any views expressed, or products or services offered.

In: Evaluating Online Learning
Editor: Arthur T. Weston, pp. 103-106
ISBN 978-1-60741-107-9

APPENDIX B: RESEARCH METHODOLOGY

The research approach underlying this guide is a combination of case study methodology and benchmarking of best practices. used in businesses worldwide as they seek to continuously improve their operations, benchmarking has more recently been applied to education for identifying promising practices. Benchmarking is a structured, efficient process that targets key operations and identifies promising practices in relationship to traditional practice, previous practice at the selected sites (lessons learned), and local outcome data. the methodology is further explained in a background document,[30] which lays out the justification for identifying promising practices based on four sources of rigor in the approach:

- theory and research base
- Expert review
- Site evidence of effectiveness
- Systematic field research and cross-site analysis

The steps of the research process were: defining a study scope; seeking input from experts to refine the scope and inform site selection criteria; screening potential sites; selecting sites to study; conducting site interviews, visits, or both; collecting and analyzing data to write case reports; and writing a user-friendly guide.

SITE SELECTION CRITERIA AND PROCESS

In this guide, the term "online learning program" is used to describe a range of education programs and settings in the K–12 arena, including distance learning courses offered by universities, private providers, or teachers at other schools; stand-alone "virtual schools" that provide students with a full range of online courses and services; and Web portals that provide teachers, parents, and students with a variety of online tools and supplementary education materials. as a first step in the study underlying this guide, researchers compiled a list of evaluations of K–12 online programs that had been conducted by external evaluators, research organizations, foundations, and program leaders. this initial list, compiled via Web and document searches, was expanded through referrals from a six-member advisory group and other knowledgeable experts in the field. Forty organizations and programs were on the final list for consideration.

A matrix of selection criteria was drafted and revised based on feedback from advisors. the three quality criteria were:

- the evaluation included multiple outcome easures, including student achievement.
- the findings from the evaluation were widely communicated to key stakeholders of the program being studied.
- Program leaders acted on evaluation results.

Researchers then rated each potential site on these three criteria, using publicly available information, review of evaluation reports, and gap- filling interviews with program leaders. all the included sites scored at least six of the possible nine points across these three criteria.

Because the goal of the publication was to showcase a variety of types of evaluations, the potential sites were coded as to such additional characteristics as internal vs. external evaluator, type of evaluation design, type of online learning program, organization unit: district or state, and stage of maturity. the final selection was made to draw from as wide a range on these characteristics as possible while keeping the quality criteria high, as described above.

DATA COLLECTION

Data were collected through a combination of on-site and virtual visits. Because the program sites themselves were not brick-and-mortar, phone interviews were generally sufficient and cost-effective. But some site visits were conducted face-to-face to ensure access to all available information. Semistructured interviews were conducted with program leaders, other key program staff, and evaluators. Key interviews were tape recorded to ensure lively descriptions and quotes using natural language. While conducting the case studies, staff also obtained copies of local documents, including evaluation reports and plans documenting use of evaluation findings.

Program leaders and evaluators were asked to:

- describe the rationale behind the evaluation and, if applicable, the criteria for choosing an external evaluator;
- Explain the challenges and obstacles that were faced throughout the evaluation process, and how they were addressed;
- tell how the study design was affected by available resources;
- If the evaluation was conducted externally, describe the relationship between the program and contractor;
- Provide the framework used to design and implement the evaluation;
- tell how the appropriate measures or indicators were established;
- Explain how the indicators are aligned to local, state, and/or national standards, as well as program goals;
- describe the data collection tools;
- Explain the methods used for managing and securing data;
- describe how data were interpreted and reported; and
- Share improvements made in program services and the evaluation process.

ANALYSIS AND REPORTING

A case report was written about each program and its evaluation and reviewed by program leaders and evaluators for accuracy. drawing from these case reports, program and evaluation documentation, and interview transcripts, the project team identified common themes about the challenges faced over the course of the evaluations and what contributed to the success of the evaluations. this cross-site analysis built on both the research literature and on emerging patterns in the data.

This descriptive research process suggests promising practices—ways to do things that others have found helpful, lessons they have learned— and offers practical how-to guidance. this is not the kind of experimental research that can yield valid causal claims about what works. Readers should judge for themselves the merits of these practices, based on their understanding of why they should work, how they fit the local context, and what happens when they actually try them. also, readers should understand that these descriptions do not constitute an endorsement of specific practices or products.

USING THE GUIDE

Ultimately, readers of this guide will need to select, adapt, and implement practices that meet their individual needs and contexts. Evaluators of online programs, whether internal or external, may continue to study the issues identified in this guide, using the ideas and practices and, indeed, the challenges, from these program evaluations as a springboard for further discussion and exploration. In this way, a pool of promising practices will grow, and program leaders and evaluators alike can work together toward finding increasingly effective approaches to evaluating online learning programs.

In: Evaluating Online Learning
Editor: Arthur T. Weston, pp. 107-108
ISBN 978-1-60741-107-9

GLOSSARY OF COMMON EVALUATION TERMS

Control group refers to the population of subjects (e.g., students) who do not receive or participate in the treatment being studied (e.g., an online class) but whose performance or other outcomes are being compared to those of students who will receive or participate in the treatment.

Formative evaluations generate information aimed at helping program stakeholders better understand a program or its participants, often by examining the delivery or implementation of a program. Findings from these evaluations are generally used to make program improvements or influence future decisions.

Hierarchical linear modeling, also called multi-level modeling, is used for the same purpose as regression analysis—to understand what factors are the best predictors of an outcome, such as a test score. But researchers use hierarchical linear modeling to take into account factors at different levels of an education system, such as the characteristics of the class or school in which students are situated. Hierarchical linear modeling helps statisticians address the fact that students are generally not grouped randomly within classes or schools and that classroom- and school-level factors are often related to student outcomes.

Quasi-experiments are experimental studies in which subjects are not assigned at random to treatment and control groups, as with RCts (see below). Quasi-experimental studies may be used, for example, when controlled trials are infeasible (e.g., when evaluators cannot assign students randomly to participate in a treatment) or are considered too expensive. according to the u.S. department of Education's What Works Clearinghouse, strong evidence of a program's effectiveness can be obtained from a quasi- experimental study based on one of three designs: one that "equates" treatment and control groups, either by matching groups based on key characteristics of participants or by using statistical methods to account for differences between groups; one that employs a discontinuity design in which participants are assigned to the treatment and control groups based on a cutoff score on a pretreatment measure that typically assesses need or merit; or one that uses a "single-case design" involving repeated measurement of a single subject (e.g., a student or a classroom) in different conditions or phases over time.[31]

Randomized controlled trials (RCTs) are experimental studies that randomly assign some study participants to receive a treatment (e.g., participation in a class or program) and others to not receive the treatment. this latter is known as the control group. In an RCt, evaluators compare the outcomes (e.g., test scores) of the treatment group with those of the control group; these results are used to determine the effectiveness of the treatment. RCts can provide strong evidence of a program's effectiveness.

Regression analysis is a statistical technique used in research to determine the factors or characteristics (e.g., gender, family income level, whether a student participated in a particular program) that are the best predictors of an outcome. Regression analyses help statisticians isolate the relationships between individual factors and an outcome and, thus, are useful when trying to understand the relationship of a program to student achievement.

Summative evaluations examine the effects or outcomes of a program. Findings from these evaluations are generally used to assess how well a program is meeting its stated goals.

Treatment group refers to the population of subjects (in this case, students) who receive or participate in the treatment being studied (e.g., an online class).

In: Evaluating Online Learning
Editor: Arthur T. Weston, pp. 107-108
ISBN 978-1-60741-107-9

NOTES

[1] For further description and discussion of online resources, online courses, virtual schools, virtual classrooms, and virtual schooling, see Cathy Cavanaugh and Robert L. Blomeyer, eds., *What Works in K–12 Online Learning* (Eugene, OR: International Society for Technology in Education, December 2007).

[2] John Watson and Jennifer Ryan, *Keeping Pace with K–12 Online Learning: A Review of State-Level Policy and Practice* (November 2007). Available online from the North American Council for Online Learning (NACOL) at http://www.nacol.org (last accessed June 27, 2008).

[3] Run by the nonprofit College Board, the Advanced Placement program offers college-level course work to high school students. Many institutions of higher education offer college credits to students who take AP courses.

[4] Liz Pape, Mickey Revenaugh, John Watson, and Matthew Wicks, "Measuring Outcomes in K-12 Online Education Programs: The Need for CommonMetrics." *Distance Learning* 3, no. 3 (2006): 58.

[5] Ibid, p. 58.

[6] Cathy Cavanaugh, Kathy Jo Gillan, Jeff Kromrey, Melinda Hess, and Robert L. Blomeyer, *The Effects of Distance Education on K–12 Student Outcomes: A Meta-analysis* (Naperville, IL: North Central Regional Educational Laboratory, 2004), p. 25. Available at http://www.ncrel.org/tech/distance/ k12distance. pdf (last accessed June 30, 2008).

[7] Available online at http://www.wisconsin eschool.net (last accessed Feb. 15, 2008).

[8] The U.S. Department of Education does not mandate or prescribe particular curricula or lesson plans. The information in this table was provided by the identified site or program and is included here as an illustration of only one of many resources that educators may find helpful and use at their option. The Department cannot ensure its accuracy. Furthermore, the inclusion of

information in this table does not reflect the relevance, timeliness, or completeness of this information; nor is it intended to endorse any views, approaches, products, or services mentioned in the table.

[9] Registration is required to access the OPPI and some consultation with its developers may be needed to implement the process fully.

[10] Laura M. O'Dwyer, Rebecca Carey, and Glenn Kleiman, "A Study of the Effectiveness of the Louisiana Algebra I Online Course," *Journal of Research on Technology in Education* 39, no. 3 (2007): 289–306.

[11] Laura M. O'Dwyer, Rebecca Carey, and Glenn Kleiman, "The Louisiana Algebra I Online Initiative as a Model for Teacher Professional Development: Examining Teacher Experiences," *Journal of Asynchronous Technologies* 11, no. 3 (September 2007).

[12] Debra Friedman, *Evaluation of the First Phase of the Washington Digital Learning Commons: Critical Reflections on the First Year* (Seattle, WA: Digital Learning Commons, 2004). Available at http://www.learningcommons.org/about/files/Year OneEvaluation.pdf (last accessed Apr. 14, 2008).

[13] The U.S. Department of Education does not mandate or prescribe particular curricula or lesson plans. The information in this figure was provided by the identified site or program and is included here as an illustration of only one of many resources that educators may find helpful and use at their option. The Department cannot ensure its accuracy. Furthermore, the inclusion of information in this figure does not reflect the relevance, timeliness, or completeness of this information; nor is it intended to endorse any views, approaches, products, or services mentioned in the figure.

[14] Credit recovery is a way to "recover" credit for a course that a student took previously but without successfully earning academic credit. Credit recovery programs have a primary focus of helping students stay in school and accumulate the credits needed to graduate.

[15] Podcasts are audio files that are distributed via the Internet, which can be played back on computers to augment classroom lessons.

[16] Blogs are regularly updated Web sites that usually provide ongoing information on a particular topic or serve as personal diaries, and allow readers to leave their own comments.

[17] Tom Clark and Elizabeth Oyer, *Ensuring Learner Success in CPS/VHS Courses: 2004–05 Report and Recommendations* (Chicago: TA Consulting & Evaluation Solutions, 2006).

[18] For more information on *FERPA*, see http://www.ed.gov/policy/gen/guid/fpco/ferpa/index.html.

[19] The U.S. Department of Education does not mandate or prescribe particular curricula or lesson plans. The information in this figure was provided by the identified site or program and is included here as an illustration of only one of many resources that educators may find helpful and use at their option. The Department cannot ensure its accuracy. Furthermore, the inclusion of information in this figure does not reflect the relevance, timeliness, or completeness of this information; nor is it intended to endorse any views, approaches, products, or services mentioned in the figure.

[20] Michael Long and Helene Jennings, *Maryland Public Television's Pathways to Freedom Electronic Field Trip: A Randomized Controlled Trial Study of Effectiveness* (Calverton, MD: Macro International, 2005).

[21] Laura M. O'Dwyer, Rebecca Carey, and Glenn Kleiman, "A Study of the Effectiveness of the Louisiana Algebra I Online Course," *Journal of Research on Technology in Education* 39, no. 3 (2007): 289–306.

[22] Advancement Via Individual Determination (AVID) is a program that prepares 4th through 12th grade students for four-year college eligibility.

[23] The U.S. Department of Education does not mandate or prescribe particular curricula or lesson plans. The information in this table was provided by the identified site or program and is included here as an illustration of only one of many resources that educators may find helpful and use at their option. The Department cannot ensure its accuracy. Furthermore, the inclusion of information in this table does not reflect the relevance, timeliness, or completeness of this information; nor is it intended to endorse any views, approaches, products, or services mentioned in the table.

[24] Run by the nonprofit College Board, the Advanced Placement program offers college-level course work to high school students. Many institutions of higher education offer college credits to students who take AP courses.

[25] Rosina Smith, Tom Clark, and Robert L. Blomeyer, *A Synthesis of New Research on K–12 Online Learning* (Naperville, IL: Learning Point Associates, November 2005). Available at http://www.ncrel.org/tech/synthesis/synthesis.pdf (last accessed Mar. 5, 2008).

[26] Cathy Cavanaugh, Kathy Jo Gillan, Jeff Kromrey, Melinda Hess, and Robert L. Blomeyer, *The Effects of Distance Education on K–12 Student Outcomes: A Meta-analysis* (Naperville, IL: North Central Regional Educational Laboratory, 2004). Available at http:// www.ncrel.org/tech/distance/k12distance.pdf (last accessed June 27, 2008).

[27] Gerald Stahler, "Improving the Quality of Evaluations of Federal Human Services Demonstration Programs," *Evaluation and Program Planning* 18 (1995): 129–141.

[28] Run by the nonprofit College Board, the Advanced Placement program offers college-level course work to high school students. Many institutions of higher education offer college credits to students who take AP courses.

[29] Title I of the *Elementary and Secondary Education Act* (ESEA) is intended to provide financial assistance to local education agencies and schools with high numbers or percentages of economically disadvantaged children to help ensure all children meet state academic standards.

[30] Nikola Filby, "Approach to Methodological Rigor in the Innovation Guides," working paper, WestEd, San Francisco, 2006.

[31] What Works Clearinghouse, "Evidence Standards for Reviewing Studies" (Washington, D.C.: u.S. Department of Education, 2006), p. 1. Available at http://ies.ed.gov/ncee/wwc/pdf/study_standards_ final.pdf (last accessed Mar. 24, 2008).

INDEX

D

E

F

G

H

I

N

O

P

Q

R

S

T